NEEDLE WORK

A Selected Bibliography
with Special Reference to
Embroidery and Needlepoint

CATHERINE J. SESTAY

THE SCARECROW PRESS, INC.
Metuchen, N.J., & London • 1982

Library of Congress Cataloging in Publication Data

Sestay, Catherine J.
   Needlework : a selected bibliography with special
reference to embroidery and needlepoint.

   Includes indexes.
   1. Needlework--Bibliography. 2. Embroidery--
Bibliography. 3. Canvas embroidery--Bibliography.
I. Title.
Z6153.N43S47   016.74644   [TT750]   82-5806
ISBN 0-8108-1554-0   AACR2

CONTENTS

★

During the last decade, arts and crafts in general and different types of needlework in particular gained wide popularity. As a result of the demand, books were published in increasing number. However, no bibliography has been published so far to assist the needleworker in the selection of material.

With the present volume, I would like to fill this gap and provide guidance to those who are interested in needlework and are looking for instruction, patterns, or specific varieties of the craft.

In the selection of material, I have tried to limit the list to two distinctive type of needlework: embroidery and canvaswork (often called needlepoint). This decision was based on the fact that these are the two most popular forms of needlework, and consequently the greatest number of books has been published on these subjects.

Embroidery is the threaded decoration of material with one or more stitches placed to form a design. One of the oldest known crafts, it could well be called painting with thread. The first embroideries were probably done with needle of bone and threads of hair. They possibly inspired other forms of graphic decoration, such as the prehistoric cave painting. The American Indians had beautiful embroideries done on doeskin with dyed quills. Embroidery, which has been called the art of all nations, reflects, like other graphic arts, the psychological and sociological times and tastes of the people. It has passed through periods of great importance and popularity and through periods of relatively small economical and social value. But it has always been a popular home craft and it has never fallen into total disuse.

Embroidery stitches are difficult to classify because there are so many of them, different kinds used in many different ways. Running, back, and stem stitches are for the most part linear; chain and split stitches can be used for both lines and filled-in areas.

In this bibliography are several books that use the term "crewel" embroidery. Crewel does not refer to any particular type of work or stitch. It is embroidery done with wool (usually three-ply), although recently the use of this word is changing and coming to mean a type of embroidery with the filled-in look of crewel, no matter what thread is used. It is very popular today, and so many books have been published dealing with that type of embroidery.

One basic pattern deserves special attention. It is the cross-stitch, consisting of two slanted stitches that form an x. In the very simplicity of the stitch lies much of its charm. One stitch crosses over another again and again in neat geometric rows to form delicate patterns, figures, and pictorial scenes. We can find the richest and most varied patterns of cross-stitch in the East European countries.

Needlepoint (sometimes called canvas embroidery) is an embroidery stitch worked with a needle over the exact threads of a canvas to make itself into a fabric. It differs from "freestyle" embroidery, which does not depend on a needle going into an exact hole to complete a stitch.

Until the seventeenth century, needlepoint was worked over fine linen. With the introduction of upholstered furniture and the need for durable support, a coarse but strong and evenly woven canvas was developed. Today, there are two types of canvases available. "Penelope," available mostly in Europe, is a double-threaded canvas. "Mono," most popular in the United States, is a single-threaded canvas with evenly spaced warp and woof threads. All canvas is measured by the number of stitches in one running inch. These canvas sizes determine the type of needlepoint being done: sixteen or more stitches to the inch is referred to as "petit-point"; fewer than sixteen stitches to the inch is "gross-point." While there are many stitches that can be worked on a canvas, needlepoint uses one particular, diagonal, stitch.

Another stitch, not diagonal but vertical, is <u>bargello</u>, also called Florentine canvaswork, or Hungarian point. In Colonial America, its name was "Irish stitch" or "flame stitch." It consists of flat vertical stitches laid parallel with the canvas weave rather than crossing the intersections diagonally as in needlepoint. By gradating tones of the same color, or in contrasting colors, one can achieve a striking effect.

Needlepoint is often worked on canvas where the pattern (picture, face, etc.) is preprinted, making the task of the needleworker much easier. A variety of techniques can be used to transpose a pattern onto the canvas, and these are usually discussed in the needlepoint books. Many other types of needlework are done on a "clear" canvas--by means of charts or, in the case of bargello, simply by counting the threads.

The following list of books represent many variations of needlepoint and bargello patterns. Since it is a distinctive type of canvaswork, books about bargello are listed separately in the index, as a subdivision of needlepoint.

I have also included in my list several books that discuss other types of needlework besides embroidery and needlepoint. Without these items, the list would be very meager, since needlework books in many cases--at least fifty percent of the publications--are not limited to one single craft or technique, but incorporate several of them.

A substantial percentage of books in this bibliography are so-called "workbooks," or how-to books, in which the user is presented with specific instructions. These instructions are either general, referring to certain technical problems, or directed toward specific projects described in the book. My list also includes several volumes that can be called "pattern books"--works that contain no (or minimal) instructions but rather emphasize designs. These patterns can be copied or used for further design by different crafts, needlework being one of them. Finally, the list includes a few books that could be characterized as being historical treatment. They discuss the history, social significance, and role of needlework in different societies and countries.

I sincerely hope that this volume will be a useful tool to help needleworkers of all ages and at all levels to select material that they require.

How to use the bibliography

Entries are listed in alphabetical order by author. The number assigned to each entry is the reference number for the indexes.

   Items 1 through 52 are reference books. Reference books in the field of needlework are usually not limited to the two types of stitch emphasized in this bibliography. I have, however, included several of these volumes because of their extensive treatment of embroidery and needlepoint. Furthermore, reference works, unlike other volumes listed here, are not marked according to level of difficulty, since many of them are not workbooks, or are intended for all levels, from beginners to the more experienced. The dividing line between reference and nonreference books in this field is somewhat arbitrary: certain books could be classified in either category. I have tried to limit my reference list to those volumes that cover the same period as the nonreference items--that is, the 1970s.

   The level of difficulty is marked by a code in brackets after each entry:

   [A] beginner
   [B] intermediate
   [C] advanced
   [D] all levels, from beginner to advanced.

NEEDLEWORK ★ A Selected Bibliography

1 ● Ambuter, Carolyn. Carolyn Ambuter's Complete Book of Needlepoint; With the Most Comprehensive, Easiest-to-Use Dictionary of Stitches Ever Compiled. Illustrated by Patti Baker Russell; photographs by Fred Sampen. New York: Crowell, 1972. 147p. [REF]

The list of stitches presented here seems to be comprehensive. The descriptions are clear, and the illustrations are enlarged for easy understanding. The photographs of the finished projects, however, are often fuzzy, and the lack of color in most of them makes it difficult to grasp the real impact of the work. An alphabet sampler, composed of different stitches, is included.

2 ● Anchor Manual of Needlework. London: Batsford; Boston: Branford, 1958. 499p. [REF]

A complete encyclopedia of needlework techniques. Considerable space is devoted to various embroidery methods, besides lacemaking, macrame, crochet, and knitting. The chapter on "various types of embroidery" covers a range of Italian techniques--e.g., embroidery in gold and with beads and sequins. Detailed instructions with photographs (few in color) and drawings are included. The volume can be used either as a workbook or as a reference book.

3 ● Arco Encyclopedia of Embroidery Stitches. New York: Arco, 1979. 336p. [REF]

This encyclopedic index covers 500 embroidery stitches, grouped in thirteen categories. An alphabetical index provides page references to each stitch. Line diagrams explain step-by-step methods. Six color plates and black-and-white illustrations show the working of more complex stitches. A useful reference work.

4 ● The Blandford Book of Traditional Handicrafts. Edited by John Rome. London: Blandford; dist. by Sterling, 1981. 169p. [REF]

The "traditional" crafts described in this book comprise those practiced by members of the Dorset (England) Arts and Crafts Society. The twelve crafts treated here do not necessarily represent all of the so-called traditional crafts. Among the missing are woodworking, knitting, and weaving. Each chapter, covering a different craft, is written by a specialist and features a brief history, basic techniques, necessary materials and equipment, and a few projects. Both photographs and illustrations are clear and easy to understand. A basic reference book for beginners who need simple instructions.

5 ● Bolton, Ethel Stanwood, and Eva Johnston Coe. American Samplers. New York: Weathervane, 1973. 416p. [REF]

This book comprises over 2, 500 descriptions of samplers with nearly 400 pictures, plus examination of over 300 samplers from the seventeenth and eighteenth centuries. For illustrations, the authors chose those that represent a variety of styles and stitches and that have historical interest. This book is an unusual chronological history of the American sampler. The material is given in a catalog form--description, place, date, name of the maker, and present owner (often a museum or historical collection). Originally published fifty-two years ago, this standard reference work will be of value not only to needleworkers but to museum curators and historians.

6 ● Bucher, Jo. Complete Guide to Creative Needlepoint. Des Moines: Creative Home Library/Meredith, 1973. 324p. [REF]

One of the most extensive encyclopedias of needlework, this volume includes 218 stitches, or their variations, which are clearly explained and accompanied by clear diagrams, black-and-white illustrations, and some color plates. Instructions on various techniques, more extensive than in the average book, discuss special needlepoint effects, attractive finishing touches for the projects, and canvas, needle, and yarn requirements.

7 ● Bucher, Jo. The Complete Guide to Embroidery Stitches and Crewel. Des Moines: Creative Home Library/Meredith, 1971. 353p. [REF]

After a short introductory chapter about the techniques of needlework, the main body of the book presents a dictionary of stitches. They are listed in alphabetical order, explained and illustrated with clear diagrams. The appendix contains terms used in embroidery, cross-references to stitch names, suggested use of stitches, and a list of suppliers. A few color plates show finished projects. A good dictionary of all kinds of embroidery stitches.

8 ● Butler, Winifred. The Complete Book of Needlework and Embroidery. New York: Castle, 1966, 196p. [REF]

Published originally in England as Needlework and Embroidery, this book includes not only every kind of decorative needlecraft--crewel embroidery, appliqué, needlepoint, smocking, patchwork, etc.--but also the essential techniques of home sewing, upholstery, slipcover- and rugmaking, knitting, and crochet. Everything is clearly explained in progressive diagrams and easy-to-follow instructions. A compact book, containing a wealth of information. The photographs are only in black-and-white, lessening the attractiveness of the volume.

9 ● Caulfeild, S. F. A., and Blanche C. Saward. The Dictionary of Needlework; An Encyclopaedia of Artistic, Plain and Fancy Needlework. London: Gill, 1882. Repr. Detroit: Singing Tree, 1971. 528p. [REF]

10 ● Caulfeild, S. F. A., and Blanche C. Saward. Encyclo-

paedia of Victorian Needlework: Dictionary of Needlework. 2nd ed. London: Cowan, 1887. Repr.
New York: Dover, 1972. 2 vols. [REF]

These reprints of the first and the second edition
of a nineteenth-century classic provide descriptions and illustrations of all types of "plain and fancy" needlework: sewing, knitting, crochet, embroidery, needlepoint, and so on.
The title page of the original works (both editions) describes
the contents: "An encyclopaedia of artistic, plain and fancy
needlework, dealing fully with the details of all the stitches
employed, the method of working, the materials used, the
meaning of technical terms, and where necessary, tracing
the origin and history of the various works described."
The Singing Tree reprint of the first edition, in a single
hardcover volume, includes the original advertisements.
The two-volume Dover paperback reprint of the second edition, illustrated with several color plates, offers a 158-page supplement with line drawings of household objects, appropriate
for various needlework projects.

11 ● Christensen, Jo Ippolito. The Needlepoint Book: 303
Stitches with Patterns and Projects. Englewood
Cliffs, N.J.: Prentice-Hall, 1976. 384p. [REF]

This comprehensive guide to needlework describes
over 300 separate needlepoint stitches and contains more
than 1,000 illustrations (500 black-and-white photographs,
500 line drawings, and 48 colored pictures). The author
provides samplers for each stitch and a chart of stitch characteristics explaining why each is good (or bad) for borders,
designs, accents, and so on. Besides the stitches, she provides the reader with instructions on how to choose the canvas, yarn, and design, with an eye to color, proportion,
and balance. Instructions for finishing the project are also
included. A good bibliography and outlined drawings of the
projects are appended.

12 ● Clabburn, Pamela. The Needleworker's Dictionary.
New York: Morrow, 1976. 296p. [REF]

This book provides complete information on two
types of needlework; embroidery and needlepoint. Nearly
2,000 alphabetically arranged entries offer clear and easy-
to-read definitions, with illustrations and detailed line draw-

ings. There are forty full-page color photographs of needlework items and many black-and-white drawings. Entries
cover stitches, motifs, countries, types of yarns, designs,
terminology, organizations, types of embroidery, and people.
The 300-item bibliography gives author, title, date, and place
of publication for most entries. This is followed by a "select list of the museums and collections where textiles can
be seen." An excellent reference book on the two most popular types of needlework.

13 ● Davis, Mildred J. The Art of Crewel Embroidery.
New York: Bonanza, 1962. 224p. [REF]

   After surveying the history and development of crewel embroidery, Davis covers all aspects of the technique.
The stitches and designs are fully illustrated with drawings
or photographs. The second part of the book presents design units for further experimentation and also four advanced designs. Some 156 floral and animal patterns are
included in the design units.

14 ● Dillmont, Therese de. The Complete Encyclopedia of
Needlework. 2nd ed. Philadelphia: Running Press,
1978. 700p. [REF]

   A translation of the original nineteenth-century work,
a classic in the field of needlework, this encyclopedia is
most useful to the experienced needleworker. It is a comprehensive guide to the various forms of needlecraft, but
the lack of an index is definitely a drawback. The table of
contents is thorough, however, and the arrangement is rea-
sonable, moving from plain sewing through various forms
of embroidery to needlepoint, tapestry, macrame, lacemaking, and the trims. The final section includes directions on
pattern transfer, adaptations, and cleaning hints.

15 ● Endacott, Violet M. Design in Embroidery. New
York: Macmillan, 1964. 183p. [REF]

   An encylcopedic treatment of embroidery. Each
type (canvaswork, cross-stitch, darning, double-running) is
represented in a short but detailed chapter, which discusses
probable origin, techniques, and applications of the particular type of work. Practical aspects are also discussed

(tools, materials, finishing, restoring, etc.). Black-and-blue illustrations add to the value of this useful reference tool.

16 ● Family Circle Creative Needlecrafts. By the Editors
     of Family Circle. Edited by Rosemary Drysdale.
     Englewood Cliffs, N.J.: Columbia House; dist. by
     Prentice-Hall, 1979. 240p. [REF]

The editors of Family Circle magazine have chosen many of their best projects for this encyclopedic treatment, ranging over a great variety of techniques: needlepoint, bargello, embroidery, appliqué, patchwork, macrame, rug-hooking, knitting, crocheting, and so on. The instructions are clear, accompanied by photographs of the finished projects, mostly in black-and-white, some in color. More color photographs would have better served the reader, since the black-and-white illustrations are not always clear. The last chapters discuss technical aspects of the various techniques, in addition to fundamentals of enlarging and reducing designs.

17 ● The Family Creative Workshop. The Golden Book of
     Hand and Needle Arts. New York: Golden Press,
     1977. 160p. [REF]

This book covers a great variety of needlework techniques. Each is illustrated with a project. The finished article is shown in color together with some details of the work. Since so many techniques are discussed, there is no room left for in-depth instructions. The volume can, however, serve as a handy reference work.

18 ● Fanning, Robbie and Tony. Here and Now; Stitchery
     from Other Times and Places. New York: Butter-
     ick, 1978. 200p. [REF]

This encyclopedic treatment of embroidery from all over the world is divided into five chapters, according to material--e.g., skins, linen, cotton, wool, or silk. Within each chapter, countries are represented by their characteristic type of embroidery in the form of a project, giving the working instructions for each, with charts and pictures. There are twenty-six projects in all, providing the user with a large selection of ideas and techniques.

19 ● The Golden Hands Complete Book of Embroidery. New York: Random House, 1973. 286p. [REF]

This British encyclopedia, reprinted for American users, offers an extensive treatment of embroidery, both traditional and modern--including bargello, needlepoint, crewel, appliqué, cross-stitch, and other techniques. Every aspect is fully covered, including such subjects as how to create collector's pieces and how to use unusual materials (leather, beads, etc.). The book is richly illustrated with color pictures, photographs, and charts. Provides hundreds of ideas for both beginners and expert needleworkers.

20 ● Gostelow, Mary. The Complete International Book of Embroidery. New York: Simon and Schuster, 1977. 288p. [REF]

This volume is an extraordinary collection of needlework from all over the world. The text is arranged by continent and within continent by country. The projects are illustrated in color, with some details. Each project is a representative sample. The author describes the history and special characteristics of the embroidery of each nation. Some of the countries are represented by motifs, others by actual projects. An unusual collection of embroidery designs, and ready-reference source for the embroidery around the world.

21 ● Gostelow, Mary. Mary Gostelow's Embroidery Book. New York: Dutton, 1978. 247p. [REF]

A complete and practical reference book for both beginners and the more experienced. Each type of embroidery stitch is explained in a separate chapter, illustrated with diagrams and charts, and accompanied by an easy-to-understand text. Simple stitches and those that are related are grouped for easier understanding. Six attractive and diverse projects, designed by the author, are completely explained and are illustrated in color. A bibliography and a comprehensive index for cross-references are included. An excellent guide and reference book.

22 ● Gostelow, Mary. A World of Embroidery. New York: Scribner, 1975. 512p. [REF]

A complete reference book that will be of great interest to embroiderers, artists, and browsers. The first
part, entitled "The Nations," describes the embroidery of
seventy-three countries, with historical background for each.
Part II, "Stitchery," contains diagrams for 177 stitches in
alphabetical order. There are many illustrations, both in
black-and-white and in color, and a twelve-page list of "Suggested Reference Material."

23 ● Groves, Sylvia. A History of Needlework Tools and
        Accessories. London: Country Life, 1966. 136p.
        [REF]

This unusual book deals with a subject not covered
anywhere else in the literature: the tools and accessories
that have been used in needlework throughout the centuries.
The volume presents fascinating material for the social his-
torian and a challange for the collector. More than 200
black-and-white illustrations--some from museums in the
United States and Europe--enhance the usefulness of this
valuable book.

24 ● Guild, Vera P. The Good Housekeeping New, Complete
        Book of Needlecraft. 2nd ed. New York: Good
        Housekeeping Books, 1971. 548p. [REF]

A complete encyclopedia of all kinds of needlework,
covering thirteen techniques, among them basic sewing and
machine embroidery. Each chapter discusses the basic techniques and stitches, and presents several projects with exact
instructions and photographs (some in color). A useful reference volume.

25 ● Ireys, Katherine. The Encyclopedia of Canvas Em-
        broidery Stitch Patterns. New York: Crowell,
        1972. 160p. [REF]

The purpose of this book is to present "almost all
known stitch patterns for canvas embroidery." Eight pages
of black-and-white photographs show selected samples of patterns in the four main divisions used in the work: straight,
crossed, diagonal, and miscellaneous. The book contains
over 150 stitch patterns with detailed diagrams and descriptions. An excellent collection of stitches for canvas em-

broidery--i.e., needlepoint--as opposed to surface embroidery, such as crewel.

26 ● John, Edith. Creative Stitches. New York: Dover, 1967. 112p. [REF]

    The book is a compendium of about 100 stitches, presenting all variations in the field of embroidery. All stitches are illustrated with clear, easy-to-follow drawings, grouped according to certain characteristics--e.g., flat stitches, looped stitches, knotted stitches, etc. Black-and-white photographs illustrate the finished works with different stitches. A useful comprehensive dictionary.

27 ● Lammer, Jutta. The Reinhold Book of Needlecraft. New York: Van Nostrand, 1973. 296p. [REF]

    A handy reference volume for many needlework techniques: embroidery, crochet, knitting, weaving. Since this book is a translation of a work originally published in German in 1971, the chapter entitled "embroidery" discusses needlepoint, bargello, and embroidery proper. This could be confusing for American readers, but the translator apparently followed the British usage. After description of the basic techniques, a variety of projects are presented, illustrated with photographs and drawings (some in color). The volume is useful since it includes ten different techniques (crewel embroidery, crochet, knitting, tatting, weaving, rug-knotting, appliqué, patchwork, decorative machine stitching, and macrame), giving detailed instructions with samples for each method.

28 ● Lane, Rose Wilder. Woman's Day Book of American Needlework. New York: Simon and Schuster, 1963. 208p. [REF]

    This volume can serve as an encyclopedia, presenting as it does short chapters on thirteen types of needlework from crewel embroidery to rugmaking. Each technique is briefly explained and illustrated with a project, together with the necessary instructions. A useful reference volume for the experienced needleworker.

29 ● Lantz, Sherlee. A Pageant of Patterns for Needlepoint

Canvas: Centuries of Design, Textures, Stitches;
A New Exploration. Diagrams by Maggie Lane.
New York: Atheneum, 1973. 509p. [REF]

An excellent guide to the history of needlepoint and
its stitches. The author researched stitch construction and
geometric patterns from the medieval period to the nineteenth century. European, American, Near Eastern, and
Middle Eastern needlework is shown, linked by identical
motifs that are often modified but readily recognizable. Diagrams of 351 stitches are accompanied by photographs of
the patterns. Not the usual how-to book, but an encyclopedic treatment of the subject, very useful for both beginners and experienced needleworkers.

30 ● McBride, Regina. Creative Crewel Embroidery; A
Complete Illustrated Guide to Mastering the Stitches
and Exploring Designs. Garden City, N.Y.: Doubleday, 1974. 385p. [REF]

A complete guide and reference book for all aspects
of crewel embroidery, including an extensive dictionary of
stitches. These stitches are all explained, and illustrated
with drawings (a few in color). The author also presents
a short history of embroidery and instructions for further
experimentation and individual creativity. [REF]

31 ● The McCall's Book of America's Favorite Needlework
and Crafts. By the editors of McCall's Needlework
and Crafts magazine. New York: Simon and Schuster, 1976. 416p. [REF]

This compendium by the editors of McCall's magazine includes not only needlework but many other crafts:
candlemaking, stained glass, pottery, basketry, decorative
painting, and nature crafts. The directions are well presented, covering every aspect of each technique. Good photographs (some in color), graphs, and other illustrations accompany each project. The necessary equipment, materials,
size of the finished project, and all other practical aspects
are discussed. Intended more for the experienced than for
the beginner.

32 ● McCall's Embroidery Book. By the editors of McCall's

Needlework and Crafts magazine. New York: Simon
and Schuster, 1977. 287p. [REF]

A rich collection of beautiful needlework patterns
from McCall's magazine, from 1925 to the present. Com-
prising all types of designs in the field of embroidery, the
volume follows the same format as the earlier editions, including graphs and color photographs. The technical instructions are clear, precise, and easy to follow. An excellent
collection for beginner embroiderers.

33 ● McCall's Needlework Treasury; A Learn and Make Book.
By the Editors of McCall's Needlework and Crafts
magazine. New York: Random House, 1964. 390p.
[REF]

An encyclopedic treatment of many types of needlework. After an introductory chapter about our American
heritage in needlework, the different techniques--embroidery,
quilting, knitting, crochet, tatting, etc.--are discussed.
Each technique is fully explained and illustrated with drawings, charts, and photographs of the finished product. The
book contains a great variety of needlework designs, collected from the best projects of McCall's magazine.

34 ● Nichols, Marion, ed. Designs and Patterns for Embroiderers and Craftsmen; 512 Motifs from the Wm.
Briggs and Company, Ltd. "Album of Transfer Patterns." New York: Dover, 1974. 145p. [REF]

An encyclopedic treatment of designs, complete with
indexes for type of design and suggested use. This collection of turn-of-the-century embroidery designs has been edited and published especially for needleworkers who are looking for something more artistic than what is customarily
available. Although a list of basic embroidery stitches is
presented here, this is not a workbook but a source for different designs, ready to be adapted according to the creative
ability of the user.

35 ● Nichols, Marion. Encyclopedia of Embroidery Stitches,
Including Crewel. New York: Dover, 1974. 219p.
[REF]

An encyclopedic treatment of 178 stitches--classified,

clearly explained, and well taught. Featuring more than 1,400 illustrations, this is a very useful volume for those who are looking for descriptions and explanation of embroidery stitches. It can be used as a teaching aid in schools or as a ready-reference source in libraries.

36 ● Nylen, Anna-Maja. Swedish Handcraft. Translated by Anne-Charlotte Harvey. New York: Van Nostrand, 1977. 428p. [REF]

This book is not the usual how-to presentation: it also describes history and cultural milieu of the country. The crafts discussed include not only needlework but many others--e.g., rya, hand and band weaving, sprang (braiding with shed sticks), crochet and knitting, bobbin lace, metalwork, woodcrafts, and horn and bone crafts. Excellent photographs and illustrations make this volume an unusual source for every kind of Swedish handcraft. A list of sources of illustrations and a bibliography are appended.

37 ● Passadore, Wanda. The Needlework Book. New York: Simon and Schuster, 1969. 208p. [REF]

This complete reference book is divided into three main parts: embroidery, crochet, and knitting. The chapter for embroidery spans many techniques--drawnwork, canvas embroidery, tapestry, smocking, trapunto, and so on. Each technique is illustrated with color photographs, and a detailed description of the stitches is given.

38 ● Pester, Ann E. Dictionary of Needlepoint Stitches. Racine, Wis.: Western, 1978. 192p. [REF]

This work is strictly a guide to stitches. It covers 153 "plain and fancy" stitches, ranging from the basic continental stitch to the more intricate patterns. Each stitch is illustrated with one or more large, clear diagrams. The dictionary has a comprehensive index to the stitches and an adequate glossary and bibliography that lists seventeen good sources. Special features of the book are a section on "Working Left Handed" and a "Detail List." The latter is a quick-reference chart listing the stitches alphabetically, with families grouped together. Color pictures would have helped the reader to see how a variety of stitches can be blended together to create special effects.

39 ● Picken, Mary (Brooks), and others. Needlepoint for
       Everyone. New York: Harper, 1970. 215p. [REF]

       A practical guide to all phases of needlepoint, in-
cluding techniques for the left-handed. Instructions for the
various stitches are well illustrated. Suggestions are made
for choosing designs and materials, which are illustrated
with numerous examples. The author also presents photographs of historic needlepoints from Blair House, Mount
Vernon, and other sites. The book can be used as both a
workbook and as a reference source.

40 ● Reader's Digest. Complete Guide to Needlework. Ed-
       ited by Virginia Colton. Pleasantville, N.Y.: Read-
       er's Digest Association, 1979. 504p. [REF]

       A complete reference book of ten needlecrafts from
appliqué to rugmaking. Each technique is described from
start to finish, with the usual technical instructions, clear
and precise. This authoritative, comprehensive how-to guide
covers ten major needlework fields, with 2,600 photographs
and illustrations, partially in color. Every stitch, pattern,
technique, or project has fully illustrated directions, as well
as photographs of the finished product. Instructions for left-
handed people are also included. The guide is useful for
both beginners and more advanced needleworkers. One of
the best books of its kind published to date.

41 ● Ring, Betty, ed. Needlework: A Historical Survey.
       (Antiques Magazine Library.) New York: Universe,
       1975. 174p. [REF]

       A collection of more than thirty articles from the
pages of Antiques, representing a half-century of scholarly
and historical research on needlework. The articles are
grouped into five sections: English embroideries, canvaswork, schoolgirl embroideries, quilts and bedcovers, and
rugs and carpets. Both antiquarian devotees and needleworkers will benefit from this collection. The needleworker can get inspirations for different projects to create contemporary pieces. The articles are accompanied by many
photographs, but only in black-and-white.

42 ● Ryan, Mildred Graves. The Complete Encyclopedia of

Stitchery. Garden City, N.Y.: Doubleday, 1979.
689p. [REF]

The title of this volume is misleading; it is by no
means "complete" and the treatment is uneven. Over two-
thirds of the text discusses embroidery and knitting, while
the entire area of needlepoint receives only three paragraphs.
Entries within each section are arranged alphabetically, but
no index or cross-references are provided. The treatment
of embroidery and knitting is extensive, including all details
and technical instructions. The black-and-white illustrations,
however, are not clear, and for that reason only the experienced needleworker would be able to use them.

43 ● Scharf, Bella. Butterick's Fast and Easy Needlecrafts:
Over 50 Fashion and Decorating Projects You Can
Make in Less Than a Day. New York: Butterick,
1977. 200p. [REF]

The author presents fast and easy needlecraft projects for those who become frustrated with the amount of
time required for a "usual" needlecraft project. Scharf
discusses each technique in excellent detail. Needlepoint,
embroidery, macrame, appliqué, patchwork, quilting, and
crochet are featured in this compendium. Projects include
fashion accessories, afghans, pillows, planters, wall decorations, and "gift items." A metric-equivalency chart
and a short list of suppliers are provided. A very useful reference book for those who do not have the time or
patience to finish a more elaborate and time-consuming
project.

44 ● Snook, Barbara. Needlework Stitches. New York:
Crown, 1963. 127p. [REF]

A "working dictionary" for those who are interested
in the art of fine needlework. This illustrated handbook offers a range of 370 familiar and unfamiliar stitches, including unusual English and European variations. Concise directions and clear instructions make it easy for beginners
or experienced needleworkers to learn any stitch. The
stitches are grouped by working method and within each
group are arranged alphabetically. A handy reference work
for needlework stitches.

45 ● Swan, Susan Burrows. A Winterthur Guide to Amer-
    ican Needlework. New York: Crown, 1976. 144p.
    [REF]

      This guide to 117 representative examples of Amer-
ican needlework contained in the Henry Francis du Pont Winterthur Museum is also a good historical account of needlework methods used between 1650 and 1890, illustrated with
the museum pieces. All the major needlework techniques
used in America, the dates of their popularity, and the stitches used, are briefly described. Each technique is illustrated by a sample and a photograph in black-and-white or color.
The author covers many forms of needlework: canvas embroidery, crewel, quilting, knitting, and so on. Cross-references are made to the specific photographs. Three pages
of selected bibliography complete the book.

46 ● Thomas, Mary. Mary Thomas's Dictionary of Em-
    broidery Stitches. New York: Gramercy, 1935.
    234p. [REF]

      An older edition, listing 305 stitches and five old
English samplers. The stitches are arranged in alphabetical order, with clear, easy-to-follow black-and-white drawings and illustrations. The title is misleading, since the
book includes not only stitches for embroidery but all kinds
of needlepoint (canvaswork) stitches as well. A good reference book for all kind of stitches, although more recent publications present the same material in much more attractive
form.

47 ● The Time-Life Book of Needlecraft, Adapted from the
    Art of Sewing Series by the Editors of Time-Life
    Books. New York: Time-Life Books, 1976. 303p.
    [REF]

      An encyclopedia of needlework, including needlepoint,
embroidery, crochet, knitting, and lacemaking. Each chapter follows the same format--stitches and techniques, projects and patterns--accompanied by color pictures, charts,
and instructions. A rich source of basic knowledge and also
many beautiful projects.

48 ● Walzer, Mary Meister. Handbook of Needlepoint Stitch-
    es. New York: Van Nostrand, 1971. 100p. [REF]

This volume offers descriptions of ninety-eight stitches in encyclopedic fashion. Each pattern is presented with clear diagrams, detailed photographs, and concise instructions. The photographs, in black-and-white, include simple designs composed of only one or two stitches, as well as intricate designs. These more elaborate patterns illustrate how stitches can be used to stress their special textural and decorative qualities. A useful reference book for needlepoint stitches and for their many uses. Four pages of color photographs of the finished projects complete the book.

49 ● Mrs. Warren and Mrs. Pullman. Treasures in Needlework. First published in 1870. New York: Berkley, 1976. 448p. [REF]

This facsimile edition of the nineteenth-century classic in women's handicrafts is an encyclopedia of all kinds of needlework, giving instructions and description, in many cases row by row, stitch by stitch. Modern needleworkers can certainly use this book, although the small print and the fuzzy black-and-white illustrations make it not too attractive for the reader.

50 ● Wilson, Erica. Ask Erica. New York: Scribner, 1977. 127p. [REF]

This book is a low-priced, paperback encyclopedia, arranged in alphabetical order. Wilson uses a question-and-answer format to explain many stitches, as well as problems connected with needlework--e.g., blocking, cleaning, and enlarging. There are short chapters and a minimum of illustrations, though black-and-white photographs of certain patterns are presented at the end of the book. Not the usual how-to volume, but a short reference to many questions that arise in connection with needlework and that are not covered in detail by most authors.

51 ● Wilson, Erica. Crewel Embroidery. Drawings by Vladimir Kagan. New York: Scribner, 1962. 153p. [REF]

The book is designed to teach beginners how to master the fundamentals of crewel embroidery. It is also useful

to the more advanced for improving their techniques. Detailed instructions for sixty-four stitches are presented, illustrated with diagrams. Crewel embroidery, which dates
back to sixteenth-century England, is enjoying a revival today. Wilson presents in this book a wide variety of designs,
some old, some new, suitable for various projects. Because
of the detailed instructions and dictionary of stitches, the
book can be used as a reference work.

52 ● Wilson, Erica. Embroidery Book. New York: Scrib-
      ner, 1973. 374p. [REF]

      An encyclopedia that sets out "everything you want
to know about embroidery," according to the author. She
illustrates the development, techniques, and uses of seven
embroidery types--crewel, needlepoint, silk and gold thread,
blackwork, whitework, stumpwork, and appliqué. Full directions and stitch diagrams are included in each chapter,
with many illustrations of old and modern examples. Wilson
provides historic background for each type, but most im-
portant is the modern application of the techniques.

                                    End of reference section
_____

53 ● Aber, Ita. The Art of Judaic Needlework: Traditional
      and Contemporary Designs. New York: Scribner,
      1979. 150p. [C]

      The author emphasizes the ways in which contem-
porary and traditional needlework can enhance the sacred.
The designs are sophisticated, and since needlework basics
are not included only the experienced should attempt them.
The book also features a variety of Hebrew alphabets and
finishing techniques. A glossary of needlework terms and
black-and-white and some color photographs of the finished
projects (e.g., ark curtain, Sabbath bread cover) are included.

54 ● Agnew, Patience. Needlepoint for Churches. New
      York: Scribner, 1972. 127p. [D]

      This book explains how to design and work needle-

point pieces for the church. Stitches and other technical
details are illustrated with diagrams. Directions are given
on how to select appropriate designs and colors in harmony
with the subject of church symbolism. A list of churches
in the United States and England, where fine examples of
needlework may be seen and studied is included. A short
bibliography and list of suppliers is appended. An excellent
book for that specific purpose--church needlework.

55 ● Aiken, Joyce. The Portable Needlepoint Boutique.
    New York: Taplinger, 1977. 127p. [B]

     This book presents small projects that can be worked
in a minimum of time. Included are needlepoint designs for
such items as bookends, camera tote, desk set, calculator
case, hatband, change purse, and evening bag--over forty in
all. Projects are provided with full-scale patterns for easy
transfer to the canvas. Technical instructions are short,
but each project has instructions for finishing. The finished
products are shown in color pictures. A useful workbook
for small items.

56 ● Alfers, Betty. Creative Crewel. New York: Grosset
    and Dunlap, 1970. 95p. [A]

     A basic book for crewel embroidery, presenting a
variety of stitches in easy-to-understand diagrams and descriptions. Furthermore, the author gives instructions for
copying, adapting, and enlarging designs. No finished projects are presented here, but this is a handsome collection
of basic designs--flowers, animals, figures, fruits, leaves,
and so on. A good, basic treatment of embroidery for beginners.

57 ● Ambuter, Carolyn. Carolyn Ambuter's Needlepoint
    Celebrations. Illustrated by Patti Baker Russell;
    photographs by Jerry Darvin. New York: Quad-
    rangle, 1976. 221p. [D]

     This book demonstrates how to commemorate special
days in needlepoint. It includes detailed descriptions of the
projects, graphs, notes on canvas, yarn, stitches, and finishing. A list of stitches and the letters of the alphabet are
also illustrated. The designs comprise both simple projects

for beginners and more complicated ones for the experienced. Among the "celebration" patterns, the user can find the signs of the Zodiac (intended for birthdays), flowers, an American eagle pillow, an American primitive sampler, and an anniversary pillow.

58 ● Amir, Ziva. Arabesque, Decorative Needlework from the Holy Land. New York: Van Nostrand, 1977. 64p. [C]

Dedicated to the needlework of the Near East, this book is a collection of a great variety of geometric motifs following the Arabic tradition. The author studied the costumes and needlework of the area in museums and native villages. After giving a historical background, she presents over 200 patterns, with diagrams in color. These patterns are all appropriate for cross-stitch (the original stitch of the Near East) or needlepoint. They include a large number of border and scatter patterns. This is not a workbook, but a collection of specific designs. Practical applications are left to readers, according to their own needs. An interesting collection of rare and authentic embroidery patterns.

59 ● Anderson, F., ed. Crewel Embroidery. London: Octopus, 1974. 128p. [C]

Since this book is a British edition, the term "crewel embroidery" includes needlepoint and bargello. A large number of beautiful designs are presented here with various stitches. The projects include pillows, chair-covers, pictures, shirts, vests, tablecloths, and so on. Each project is described briefly, with instructions, color-key, and stitches. On the opposite page, the project is shown in a color photograph. Since basic instructions are short, this is a work only for the more experienced.

60 ● Appel, Madeleine. One-Stitch Stitchery. New York: Sterling, 1978. 48p. [A]

Ten basic stitches are explained in this book. Clear easy-to-follow illustrations, color photographs of the finished stitch, and short instructions on basic techniques make this a useful guide for beginners.

22 ★ NEEDLEWORK: A Selected Bibliography

61 ● Archer, Katherine B., and Patricia Falk Feeley. Per-
    fect Needlepoint Projects from Start to Finish. New
    York: St. Martin, 1977. 128p. [D]

   This useful workbook presents in full detail, from
start to finish, a wide range of projects, which are illustrated with over 150 line drawings and color photographs.
The articles for needlepoint include garments, travel accessories, game-boards, purses, and many more. The authors encourage readers to create their own projects, and
blank charts for this purpose are attached to the end of the
book.

62 ● Arnold, Dennis M. The Needlepoint Pattern Book.
    New York: Morrow, 1974. 183p. [D]

   The patterns in this book are designed for a wide
variety of needlepoint projects--some for the inexperienced,
others for more complex work. The designs are presented
with easy-to-copy diagrams and color plates. A concise
summary of basic needlepoint technique precedes the patterns. A list of shops and designers who contributed pieces
that appear in the book; mail-order information; and a select
bibliography are appended.

63 ● Baker, Muriel, and Margaret Lunt. Blue and White;
    The Cotton Embroideries of Rural China. New
    York: Scribner, 1977. 102p. [C]

   The authors present the folk embroideries of the
remote area of western China, very different from Peking's
elaborate silk embroidery. The majority of the pieces illustrated and described in this book were collected in the
1930s by Dr. Carl Schuster, a Sinologist and student of folk
motifs. The bulk of his collection is preserved in Basel,
Switzerland, and in the Field Museum of Natural History in
Chicago. These pieces are made of simple materials--cot-
ton thread, dyed blue with native indigo, and white cotton
cloth. The technique is almost exclusively cross-stitch.
After discussing the history and possible origin of the different motifs, the author presents the designs on photographs
and on charts at the opposite page. Basic instructions are
brief, and because of the elaborate designs, only the more experienced should use it. An unusual book about a Chinese
folk art that is not to be found in any other sources.

64 ● Baker, Muriel. A Handbook of American Crewel Embroidery. Rutland, Vt.: Tuttle, 1966. 67p. [C]

Baker devotes this book to specifically American crewel, emphasizing the difference from English crewel. After discussing the distinctive features of the American version, she describes and illustrates the various stitches and design elements. The final chapter illustrates how American crewel can be used in modern homes. Since some of the designs are quite complicated, this is only for the more experienced needleworker.

65 ● Baker, Muriel. Stumpwork; The Art of Raised Embroidery. New York: Scribner, 1978. 116p. [C]

The author describes the history and technique of the three-dimensional embroidery, called stumpwork. The author presents many original pieces from seventeenth- and eighteenth-century England, describing their origin and present location. The second part of the book is devoted to the description and explanation of stumpwork, which has rarely been used in recent times. Today, however, there is a growing interest in learning and applying this technique.

66 ● Barnes, Charles, and David P. Blake. Bargello and Related Stitchery. Great Neck, N.Y.: Hearthside, 1971. 245p. [D]

This book offers a wealth of patterns and information on every possible aspect of bargello: stitches, working techniques, shading, variations, and so on. Stitches are diagrammed and the projects fully explained. More color pictures would have made the volume more attractive.

67 ● Barnes, Charles, and David P. Blake. 120 Needlepoint Design Projects. New York: Crown, 1974. 202p. [C]

This comprehensive workbook embraces all aspects of needlepoint. The first part is devoted to materials and methods, the second to designs and charts. The designs include a great variety from traditional to modern--flowers, fruits, animals, and also the signs of the Zodiac. The charts are sometimes not very easy to follow, since differ-

ent symbols are used for color-coding. The finished works
are shown in black-and-white and also in color photographs.

68 ● Bath, Virginia Churchill. Embroidery Masterworks;
   Classic Patterns and Techniques for Contemporary
   Applications, from the Textile Collection of the Art
   Institute of Chicago. Photographs by Howard Kray-
   winkel, John Mahtesian, and Richard Brittain. Chi-
   cago: Regnery, 1972. 225p. [C]

   With the rising interest in embroidery, needleworkers are searching for new sources and unusual designs. In
this book, the author presents patterns modeled after major
embroidery works in the textile collection of the Art Institute
of Chicago. Thirty-seven patterns are illustrated, all based
on museum pieces--a Peruvian poncho shirt, Russian darnwork, Turkish ship design, and so on. Historical background is also included. The techniques of various stitches
are fully explained and illustrated. An unusual feature of
the book is that designs for little-practiced types of needlework, such as metal stumpwork and reverse appliqué, are
presented. Experienced needleworkers can find in this book
many unusual patterns.

69 ● Bath, Virginia Churchill. Needlework in American
   History; Design and Techniques. New York: Viking,
   1979. 336p. [D]

   An extensive treatment of American needlework, including all types, starting with the North American Indians,
from Colonial times to the twentieth century. The emphasis
is on embroidery, patchwork, appliqué, and knitting. The
various types of embroidery are discussed at length in separate chapters--e.g., embroidery in silk, whitework, embroidery in wool, or rugs and pile. Each technique is explained completely, with historical background. Many illustrations are included, some of them museum pieces or collector's items. An extensive bibliography rounds out the
volume.

70 ● Baxter, Nancy. Needlecraft for Home Decoration.
   Great Neck, N.Y.: Hearthside, 1971. 255p. [D]

   A comprehensive work that embraces knitting, crochet, and embroidery. After the basic instructions, about 500 projects are presented, with step-by-step instructions, charts, and pictures of the finished project. An extensive workbook, with a wealth of decorating ideas, for needleworkers at all levels.

71 ● Beaney, Jan. Embroidery; New Approaches. Photographs by Dudley Moss. London: Pelham, 1978. 96p. [C]

A modern approach to embroidery, using a variety of techniques: needlepoint, bargello, crewel, appliqué, and less usual embroidery stitches, such as bullion knots, wave stitch, and fly stitch. This book does not offer projects-- only different techniques and their combinations. At the end of the volume appear works of various artists. Most of the photos are in black-and-white, with only a few color plates. Definitely not for beginners, since some of the techniques are complicated, and technical instructions are brief.

72 ● Beautement, Margaret. Patterns from Peasant Embroidery. London: Batsford, 1968. 96p. [B]

The author offers a wide range of motifs, based on peasant embroideries from Scandinavia, Italy, Greece, Spain, and Hungary. Eighty working drawings illustrate the designs and make them available for reproduction in cross-stitch. Beautement also suggests variations and rearrangements of the original motifs. Although the motifs are suggested for the use of cross-stitch, they can be adapted to needlepoint or latch-hook. Since the text has been kept to the minimum and working instructions are brief, some experience is needed for the use of this book.

73 ● Beck, Thomasina. Embroidered Gardens. New York: Viking, 1979. 143p. [C]

This book looks at needlework in a new and exciting way. It shows how embroidery reflected contemporary gardens, and gardens in turn have been inspired by the embroiderer's needle. This idea is illustrated with engravings, woodcuts, and paintings, together with a wealth of embroideries. The book is interesting to read, but it was also intended to be used. Each major epoch of gardens and stitchery

is discussed in a separate chapter--Elizabethan, Stuart,
French, Georgian, Victorian, and modern. The author
presents certain motifs that can be copied and an entire
chapter on transforming past gardens into present embroidery, with details on blackwork, stumpwork, Berlin wool-
work (crewel), and modern canvaswork.

74 ● Beese, Pat. Embroidery for the Church. Newton
     Centre, Mass.: Branford, 1975. 104p. [D]

Offering imaginative designs for use in churches,
this book answers the question, What kind of design is ac-
ceptable? The author discusses colors, techniques, and
materials suitable for church vestments or furnishings. The
techniques are both for beginners and the more experienced.
Over 150 line drawings, photographs and color pictures of
the finished projects. A special application of needlework
for a specific purpose.

75 ● Belfer, Nancy. Designing in Stitching and Appliqué.
     Worcester, Mass.: Davis, 1972. 128p. [C]

An unusual, very modern application of embroidery
and appliqué. The author, who is a professor of textile design at the State University College at Buffalo, has written
a comprehensive book that elevates both techniques to the
level of art. Belfer stresses original designs as a means
of artistic self-expression. The book also contains a short
history of these two types of needlework. Technical instructions about materials and stitches and a large number of
photographs of the finished products are also included. Although not the usual workbook, this can be used as such by the
experienced needleworker.

76 ● Bengtsson, Gerda. Danish Floral Charted Designs.
     New York: Dover, 1980. 48p. [B]

Forty-five floral designs are presented here, twenty
in full color on the covers. The charts make it possible to
vary the size of the designs. Therefore, they can be adapted to different projects, from small pillows to bedspreads.
Instructions are given for cross-stitch, but the patterns lend
themselves easily to several forms of needlework, such as
needlepoint, rug-hooking, or other types of counted-thread
embroidery.

77 ● Bengtsson, Gerda. Gerda Bengtsson's Book of Danish
    Stitchery. Translated by Paula Hostrup-Jessen.
    New York: Van Nostrand, 1971. 135p. [C]

    In her cross-stitch embroideries of flowers and
plants, the author created a floral world that is a source
of inspiration for many embroiderers and embroidery designers. She describes the step-by-step method of transferring a design from a sketch or painting into needlework.
In the last chapter, Bengtsson gives full sewing instructions
and illustrations, some in color, for all the stitches mentioned throughout the book.

78 ● Bengtsson, Gerda. Herbs and Medicinal Plants in
    Cross-Stitch from the Danish Handcraft Guild. New
    York: Van Nostrand, 1979. 64p. [B]

    Varieties of twenty-six medicinal plants are trans-
lated into thread and linen by the author. Once displayed
on the guild's calendars, these delicate embroidered designs
have been gathered together in book format. Bengtsson provides detailed instructions about the stitches, yarn, and color,
as well as graphs. A finished example in color is presented
for each design.

79 ● Bengtsson, Gerda. U.S. State Flowers in Counted
    Cross-Stitch. New York: Van Nostrand, 1977.
    96p. [B]

    Presented in this volume are complete designs of
the flowers of each state in the Union. Forty-one designs
·(some states have the same flowers) are shown on separate
plates, with short introduction and technical instructions.
An easy-to-read diagram and color code is included for each
flower. The instructions are for cross-stitch, but they can
be adapted for needlepoint and rug-hooking. At the front
and back of the volume, we find some practical applications,
such as tablecloths, purse, picture, or pillow, of the state
flowers.

80 ● Bennett, Maggi, Sarajean Capua, and Jeanette McArthur.
    Stitchery. Hollywood, Fla.: Dukane, 1970. 32p.
    [D]

    Modern designs from simple to more sophisticated

projects, including pillows, wall hangings, decorative stitches on clothing, and other accessories. But only stitches, not complete embroidery, are presented here, applied in most cases to linenlike background materials. Full-color illustrations and short technical instructions are included with each design.

81 ● Better Homes and Gardens. <u>Embroidery.</u> Des Moines: Meredith, 1978. 96p. [C]

The material in this book is organized into six chapters, including folk embroidery, old-fashioned stitchery, designs from nature, counted-thread techniques, machine embroidery, and special techniques. Within each chapter, different projects are presented, representing various techniques. Although charts and graphs are given, they are rather small and need enlarging for actual use. Technical instructions are short and very compact; this book, therefore, should be used only by the more experienced needleworker.

82 ● Better Homes and Gardens. <u>Needlepoint.</u> Des Moines: Meredith, 1978, 96p. [D]

Different varieties of needlepoint stitches are presented here, including bargello. The projects range from simple to complicated. The descriptions are clear, and illustrations, charts, and color photographs of the finished projects are included. A glossary of stitches, a list of suppliers, and a short bibliography round out the book.

83 ● Beyer, Jinny. <u>Patchwork Patterns for All Crafts That Use Geometric Design--Quilting, Stained Glass, Mosaics, Graphics, Needlepoint, Jewelry, Weaving and Woodworking.</u> McLean, Va.: EPM, 1979. 200p. [C]

The author presents her own ingenious method to create patchwork patterns by dividing the square in many different ways, creating endless possibilities for design. Although the color plates illustrate mostly quilts, the patterns can be used by needleworkers for creating pillows, rugs, wall hangings, and so on. An unusual book, containing a wealth of information for those who like geometric designs.

84 ● Blackburn, Charles. Needlepoint Designs for Traditional Furniture. New York: Vanguard, 1980.
159p. [B]

A complete book for designing and stitching canvas
embroidery for fine furniture. The author presents explicit
directions, covering everything the reader needs to know
about materials. The graphs are clear and easy-to-read.
The stitches include bargello and needlepoint. The finished
projects are shown in color plates. A good workbook, containing many attractive designs for furniture (mostly chair
seats).

85 ● Bodi, Jack, Meg Merrill, and Catherine di Montizemo-
lo. A Gardener's Book of Needlepoint. New York:
Simon and Schuster, 1978. 154p. [C]

More than forty designs are presented here, inspired
by the brilliance of colors and shapes in flowers, fruits, and
vegetables. Designs are presented for three containers,
with interchangeable motifs. After a short technical instruction, the main body of the work includes graphs for the original designs and color pictures with the finished products.
A very original alphabet is also presented here, each letter
designed with a flower, fruit, or vegetable. A rich collection for experienced needleworkers.

86 ● Borssuck, B. 97 Needlepoint Alphabets. New York:
Arco, 1975. 144p. [D]

A pattern book of the alphabet, for needlepoint or
cross-stitch. The alphabets and numerals include Roman
and Gothic lettering in several sizes and weights, script and
italic shapes, and contemporary forms. The volume contains many patterns not to be found in most needlework books.

87 ● Borssuck, B. 1001 Designs for Needlepoint and Cross-
Stitch. New York: Arco, 1977. 180p. [D]

A rich collection of needlepoint and cross-stitch patterns, grouped according to nationality, or whether borders,
birds, animals, geometric repeat, etc. The graphs are
clear and easy to copy. The reader can find here the right
design for a great variety of projects.

88 ● Borssuck, B.   The Star of David Needlepoint Book.
New York: Arco, 1979. 128p. [D]

Borssuck presents in this volume not only the Star
of David but many other patterns for creating traditional
Jewish motifs and designs.   The book is divided into five
chapters: Star of David, alphabets, biblical themes, anti-
quity, and contemporary designs.   Within each chapter, the
projects are worked with different types of needlepoint stitches, including bargello.   The finished projects are presented
in color photographs.   A useful book for both beginners and
more experienced, serving a specific need.

89 ● Borssuck, B. , and Ann Jackson. Picture Your Dog in
Needlework.   New York: Arco, 1980.   127p. [B]

This book, which offers more than 105 graphs of
over seventy breeds, will supply the user who loves dogs
with valuable material for needlework.   The charts are
color-coded and easy to read, and there are illustrations in
black-and-white, with color photographs of the finished projects.   All the graphs may be used for any counted-thread
project, such as cross-stitch, or on canvas for petit-point
or needlepoint.   Instructions are given on how to transfer
a picture, or photograph, of dogs into different types of
needlework.

90 ● Boyles, Margaret.   American Indian Needlepoint Work-
book.   Based on materials by W. Ben Hunt and J. F.
"Buck" Burshears.   New York: Collier, 1976.   85p.
[C]

This workbook contains more than fifty graphed designs, to be either adapted or used directly.   The designs
include representative samples from many Indian tribes,
among them the Ojibwa, Sioux, Ute, and Navajo.   The projects are mostly pillows, bell-pulls, armbands, and neck-
laces.   Besides the instructions for the techniques of needlepoint, black-and-white pictures of the finished products
are appended, with some in color.   Suitable for intermediate
or experienced needleworkers.

91 ● Boyles, Margaret.   Bargello: An Explosion in Color.
New York: Macmillan, 1974.   149p. [D]

The author presents a clear introduction on how to select the canvas, yarns, and needles for bargello stitches. Her diagrams of basic needlepoint stitches that are also used in bargello are, unfortunately, blurred. The color photographs of sixty-two bargello designs are marked according to level of difficulty and accompanied by graph-paper layouts. Included are six beautiful designs for mitered bargello, an old technique shown here with a modern four-way variation. General suggestions for blocking, finishing, and mounting are offered.

92 ● Boyles, Margaret. The Margaret Boyles Bargello Workbook: A Collection of Original Designs. New York: Macmillan, 1976. 120p. [D]

Boyles again demonstrates her talent and originality in this book. She presents thirty-two new counted-canvas designs in all possible hues and tints. Lavishly illustrated with color photographs, the book should be a useful addition to both beginners and experienced needleworkers. Instructions cover every detail--material, yarn, color-selection, blocking, finishing, and so on.

93 ● Boyles, Margaret. The Margaret Boyles Book of Crewel Embroidery. New York: Simon and Schuster, 1979. 145p. [A]

The author discusses in this book only one type of embroidery, crewel, which uses a special type of wool yarn. Boyles gives instructions about all aspects of crewel embroidery for beginners, including the necessary materials, with working tips and a forty-seven-stitch dictionary. The twenty patterns are clearly described and illustrated for easy use.

94 ● Boyles, Margaret. The Margaret Boyles Book of Needle Art. New York: Harcourt, 1978. 160p. [B]

Boyles's latest book is a potpourri of techniques, including bargello (Florentine stitch), needlepoint, and crewel embroidery. The projects are varied and attractive for example, pillows, bell-pulls, minature embroideries, purses, and slippers. Each project is presented with a color graph, working instructions, and color photograph. An excellent workbook for those with some experience in needlework.

95 ● Boyles, Margaret. Margaret Boyles' Needlework Gifts
    for Special Occasions. New York: Simon and Schus-
    ter, 1981. 160p. [D]

    The projects in this book are for needlepoint and
embroidery, designed especially for holidays and other gift-
giving occasions. The sampler collection deserves special
attention, specifically the Pennsylvania Dutch wedding sampler. The instructions are clear, to the point, and accompanied by line drawings and photographs (some in color) of
the finished products. The designs are the author's adaptations of traditional needlework patterns.

96 ● Boyles, Margaret. Needlepoint Stitchery. New York:
    Macmillan, 1973. 158p. [D]

    This volume contains a collection of handsome, ver-
satile stitches, including embroidery stitches, that work on
needlepoint canvas. Basic and fancy stitches are shown in
diagrams with numbered instructions and a photograph of the
completed work. Black-and-white plates show some historic
pieces of needlepoint, while a selection of color plates am-
plifies diagrams of designs created for the book. One chapter covers bargello stitches and their use in chair coverings.
Data on blocking and finishing are given in conclusion.

97 ● Boyles, Margaret. The New Needlepoint, Stitches and
    Designs. New York: Macmillan, 1972. 152p. [B]

    A comprehensive book with some unusual features,
among them comparisons of the basic needlepoint stitch with
other stitches, and instructions on how to use embroidery
stitches on canvas. The basic stitches and parts of the finished products are illustrated very clearly, in color (almost
three-dimensional) plates. A separate chapter discusses bargello technique. Twelve designs are provided, including central motifs, borders, all-over designs, repeats, and bargel-
los. The author also discusses how to design your own
needlepoint project and how to experiment with combinations
of stitches.

98 ● Bragdon, Bill, and Jeanne Harrison. Pillow People:
    Needlepoint Designs for 40 Unusual Doll Pillows.
    New York: Hawthorn, 1976. 116p. [C]

    To change the monotony of the usual needlepoint or

bargello pillows, the authors designed forty unusual, sometimes weird-looking pillows. Although explanations for the
basic techniques are given, the book is recommended mostly for intermediate and experienced needleworkers. Each
pattern includes type of stitches, suggested yarns and colors,
and a graph outline to enlarge the design. Black-and-white
photographs of the finished product are presented for each
design. Emmet the Clown, Lolita, and Quilting Bea are
among the characters presented in this book.

99 ● Brent, Eva.   Oriental Designs in Needlepoint.   New
        York: Simon and Schuster, 1979.   128p. [C]

        Twenty patterns are presented here, based on au-
thentic works from the Orient, accompanied by easy-to-use
graphs and color charts.   Each design is adaptable to many
projects--pillows, bench covers, wall hangings, or rugs.
The author is using only two basic needlepoint stitches (continental and basket-weave), which are fully explained and illustrated.   The beautiful Chinese, Japanese, and Korean designs are quite intricate, and therefore only the experienced
should attempt them.

100 ● Brent, Eva, and Merrill, Meg.   Nature in Needle-
        point.   New York: Simon and Schuster, 1975.
        127p. [D]

        Intended for nature and animal lovers, this book
shows how to portray animals in needlepoint.   Besides the
usual information on materials, supplies, stitches, and colors, each animal design is presented in two graphs, with
suggested colors and size and type of canvas.   The patterns
are grouped by animal type and are introduced with brief
discussion of the animal.   Among the designs we find tigers,
eagles, jaguars, cheetahs, and several birds.   The final
chapter discusses finishing and sources of supplies; conclud-
ing the book are needlepoint and nature bibliographies and a
list of conservation organizations.

101 ● Bright, Sigrid.   Hardanger Embroidery; A Complete
        and Practical Course.   New York: Dover, 1978.
        32p. [C]

        An unabridged republication of an earlier work (no
date), this book is, as its subtitle states, virtually a com-

plete course on Hardanger embroidery. The name derives
from the Hardanger region of western Norway, where this
form of counted-thread embroidery originated. Clear instructions and twenty illustrations tell everything the reader
needs to know in order to master this craft. Actual projects demonstrate the practical applications of Hardanger
embroidery, with instructions and detailed photographs of
the projects.

102 ● Brinley, Rosemary. Needle Work. New York: Drake,
     1972. 95p. [C]

     A very compact book, dealing with many techniques,
such as whitework, appliqué, quilting, embroidery, smocking, and patchwork. Since too many subjects are covered
in a comparatively small volume, instructions are very short.
The techniques are illustrated with simple black-and-white
sketches.

103 ● Brown, Georgiana Harbeson. American Needlework;
     The History of Decorative Stitchery and Embroidery
     from the Late 16th to the 20th Century. New York:
     Bonanza, 1938. 128p.

     A reprint of a classic, this is a historical treat-
ment of needlework, starting with early American Indian contributions and going up to the twentieth century. The
Quakers, Pilgrims, Moravians, and other groups are covered. All types of embroidery are illustrated with original
pieces from museums or private collections. Stitches, techniques, and materials are also discussed, together with the
significance and practical applications of the works in different periods. Not a workbook, but for those who are interested in the history and development of American needlework.

104 ● Brudner, Nettie Yanoff. Painting with a Needle.
     Garden City, N.Y.: Doubleday, 1972. 192p. [C]

     The author of this book aims to treat needlepoint
as a creative art, as a form of personal self-expression.
With 140 illustrations (some in color), this book presents
different ideas, and instructions on how to adapt them to
needlework. Brudner also offers her own beautiful designs,

as well as a final chapter on how to finish, mount, and frame the needlepoint creations. To accomplish the designs, some experience in needlework is needed.

105 ● Burchette, Dorothy. Needlework Blocking and Finishing. New York: Scribner, 1974. 136p.

106 ● Burchette, Dorothy. More Needlework Blocking and Finishing. New York: Scribner, 1979. 145p.

These two volumes--the second is an expanded edition of the first--discuss in detail the many problems connected with finishing a needlework piece and incorporating it into a useful object. The author offers alternatives to the expensive prefinished kits and custom needlepoint-finishing shops. The finishing steps are described for more than thirty projects, ranging from briefcases to umbrella covers. The directions are precise, and the various steps are fully illustrated with black-and-white photographs. The author gives useful tips for saving money whenever possible. The author's goal is to obtain professional results at minimal cost. Lists of recommended products and needlework sources are appended.

107 ● Burgess, Maureen. The Pillow Book. New York: Grosset and Dunlap, 1975. 186p. [C]

A complete book about pillow making--everything the reader needs to know about shapes, patterns, fabrics, textures, fibers, fillings, and so forth. Over 150 illustrated patterns and design ideas are presented in the book for further use. The designs are grouped according to size, shape, or purpose--e.g., children's corners, fur pillows, garden and patio pillows, or pieces with a nautical air. The designs are fully explained and the finished products are shown in color photographs. Techniques include needlepoint, bargello, and embroidery, knitting, and crochet. A good, basic workbook for pillows.

108 ● Butler, Anne. Embroidery for School Children. Newton Centre, Mass.: Branford, 1969. 95p. [A]

Aimed at children aged up to thirteen, this book deals with fabrics, threads, stitches, use of materials, and simple embroidery. Parents and teachers can use this book as a guide to the production of embroidery pieces. Finished projects are not presented here; rather, the stitches and techniques are explained in detail, with basic illustrations.

109 ● Cammann, Nora. Needlepoint Designs from American Indian Art. New York: Scribner, 1973. 84p. [B]

The book presents twenty designs for pillows, stools, belts, slippers, and other articles, derived from the work of four Indian groups, those of the Southwest, the Great Plains, the Pacific Northwest and the Eastern Woodlands. Each design is illustrated in color, while diagrams and close-up black-and-white photographs show exactly how to work it. Nearly every design has been worked on canvas; only a few are crewel embroidery. Clear, easy-to-follow instructions for each project, from basic stitches to finishing touches.

110 ● Celestin, Gina. Embroider Your Clothes and Linens. Indianapolis: Bobbs-Merrill, 1978. 177p. [B]

A rich variety of needlework projects is presented here, using different embroidery stitches to decorate clothes and linens. The styles include both traditional and modern. The projects range from peasant blouse to linen tablecloth and napkins. Each design is fully explained, and illustrated with charts and pictures. Since technical instructions are short, only the more experienced should attempt these projects.

111 ● Chandler, Barbara. Step by Step Guide to Embroidery. New York: Hamlyn/America; dist. by A & W, 1976. 79p. [A]

As the title implies, the purpose of the book is to introduce the user into the techniques of embroidery, using a step-by-step method. The author starts with the essentials of basic equipment, and advances from the very simple to the more complicated stitches. Each stitch is represented with a workable project. The finished products are shown in color plates (there are also many black-and-white illustrations). A good, basic book for beginners.

112 ● Chapman, Suzanne E. Historical Floral and Animal

Designs for Embroiderers and Craftsmen. New York: Dover, 1977. 80p. [B]

According to the author, this collection of designs has been taken from historic embroidery and textiles in great museums of the world. The volume is primarily a source-book of design ideas, making no attempt to cover the technical aspects of the craft itself. Seventy-one designs are presented, and their sources are listed at the beginning of the book. The drawings are clear and easy to copy. Short instructions are included on how to transfer the designs on different materials.

113 ● Chatterton, Pauline. Gobelin Stitch Embroidery. New York: Scribner, 1980. 185p. [C]

Gobelin is a very old stitch in needlepoint that has been making a comeback in recent years. Like bargello, it covers several threads with each stitch, making the work faster and more economical. Sixteen patterns are described and explained in this book, illustrated with charts and photographs, many in color. This type of stitch is popular in Scandinavia, and many of the examples are Scandinavian in origin. A refreshing technique with endless possibilities for creating modern effects.

114 ● Christensen, Jo Ippolito, and Sonie Shapiro Ashner. Needlepoint Simplifed. New York: Sterling, 1978 (© 1971). 48p. [A]

Simple projects with basic, easy-to-follow instructions. Ten designs are described and explained from start to finish, and illustrated with diagrams, drawings, and color pictures of the finished project. A useful book for young people, or beginners.

115 ● Christensen, Jo Ippolito. Teach Yourself Needlepoint. Englewood Cliffs, N.J.: Prentice-Hall, 1978. 333p. [D]

A very thorough, basic guide, presenting all aspects of the craft. Besides the basic techniques, the author discusses other aspects of needlepoint, such as color schemes, designs, and materials. The projects are divided according to beginner, intermediate, or advanced levels. The book

contains a wealth of beautiful designs, with good, easy-to-
follow instructions, graphs and charts for copying, and many
other useful hints. The finished designs are presented in
color photographs.

116 ● Christie, Mrs. Archibald. Samplers and Stitches; A
Handbook of the Embroiderer's Art. 4th ed. New
York: Hearthside, 1959. 152p. [D]

The fourth edition of a book originally published in
1920. The author offers clear and easy-to-follow instructions for basic embroidery stitches. They are presented to
the reader by means of working diagrams, which often show
several stages of each stitch, and a series of samplers illustrate some of the uses. The author urges the reader to
start with the stitch, experiment with it, and see what type
of stitches are best suited to the project. She disapproves
of the opposite method--that is, starting with a design and
finding the best stitches for it. Her aim is to present a
textbook of modern embroidery, although not everyone would
agree with all her methods.

117 ● Chung, Young Yang. The Art of Oriental Embroidery;
History, Aesthetics and Techniques. New York:
Scribner, 1980. 183p. [C]

In this volume, which is more than the usual how-
to book, the author combines the historic, aesthetic, and
practical aspects of Oriental embroidery. Each chapter discusses the historical background, development, and use of
certain type of embroidery together with the necessary techniques to execute and finish the project. Illustrations, some
in color, accompany the text. The reader can use the material for inspiration and adapt the patterns for modern use.

118 ● Cirker, Blanche. Needlework Alphabets and Designs.
New York: Dover, 1975. 85p. [B]

A large selection of alphabets, patterns, and designs for needlepoint or cross-stitch. Twenty-seven alphabets are presented here on forty-five plates, script and
print lettering in various graphic forms, from Gothic to
modern. All designs are printed in two colors (red and
blue). The designs include geometrics, florals, crowns,

anchors, butterflies, and so on. The charts are clear and easy to copy. Since instructions are minimal, some experience is needed in using this book.

119 ● Collins, Carol Huebner. Needlepoint: A Basic Manual. Boston: Little, Brown, 1976. 172p. [B]

The author gives detailed descriptions of twenty-one stitches, including suggestions for materials, yarns, colors, and so on. Each stitch is explained with a graph, and an example of the finished product is also provided. The text follows the traditional instructions for blocking, finishing, and enlarging. A history of needlepoint, a brief bibliography, and a selected list of suppliers for materials are appended.

120 ● Cordello, Becky Stevens. Needlework Classics; Nostalgic Designs from the Butterick Archives for Decorating Clothing and Accessories. New York: Butterick, 1976. 128p. [C]

A variety of old-fashioned patterns for decoration of clothing, intended mostly for experienced needleworkers. Instructions are given not only for embroidery and needle-point but for beading, braiding, and quilting. Illustrations are in black-and-white, with some color plates. The designs are shown in full size. In a separate chapter, the designs are shown twice, once as it was used originally and then as adapted to modern dress.

121 ● Cosentino, Geraldine. Step by Step Bargello. New York: Golden Press, 1974. 64p. [B]

The charm and fascination of the bargello stitch is fully exploited in this book. A great variety of stitches and applications are described, with instructions and color photographs. The technical instructions include selection of material, color combinations, blocking, and finishing. A good workbook for bargello enthusiasts. The collection of patterns can be further used for individual designs.

122 ● Costabel-Deutsch, Eva. Full Color Floral Needlepoint Designs, Charted for Easy Use. New York: Dover, 1976. 32p. [B]

This book presents thirty-two charted designs in great variety of floral patterns. The designs, which range from the simple to the elaborate Art Deco style, are shown in full color and charted for #10 needlepoint canvas. The practical applications are left to the imagination of the user. Technical instructions are basic, and so the user needs some previous experience.

123 ● Counted Cross-Stitch Patterns and Designs. Compiled by the Swedish Handcraft Society. Translated from the Swedish by Alice Blomquist. New York: Scribner, 1981. 72p. [B]

The book presents thirty-five patterns, utilizing both the long-legged and the standard cross-stitch. For each design, the authors supply credit to the designers and instructions for materials, yarns, colors, and finishing. There are black-and-white graphs and color photographs. Four brief chapters discuss the technical aspects of the stitches. Since some of the designs are intricate and difficult to copy, experience is needed in the use of this book.

124 ● Crowell, Muriel. The Fine Art of Needlepoint. New York: Crowell, 1973. 128p. [D]

This volume contains instructions for twenty needlepoint projects; information on equipment, choice of yarn, and canvas; and discussion of design elements. Photographs of finished articles, the unworked designs, and a closeup of the stitches accompany each project. Instructions and diagrams for left-handed persons are offered for certain projects. A useful table identifies the type of stitches for general use.

125 ● Danish Handcraft Guild. Cross-Stitch Patterns in Color. Designs by Gerda Bengtsson. New York: Van Nostrand, 1974. 79p. [C]

The book is composed of Bengtsson's simple but decorative designs in the Scandinavian tradition. Each design is illustrated in full color, and on the opposite page a chart is provided for copying. The patterns fill out a square and therefore are suitable for pillows and pictures or for repetitions, according to the need of the user. Basic in-

structions are kept to the minimum--beginners will have to
look elsewhere for technical instructions.

126 ● Danish Handcraft Guild. Counted Cross-Stitch De-
      signs for Christmas. New York: Scribner, 1978.
      70 p. [C]

    This book presents original cross-stitch patterns
for Christmas. Each designs is accompanied by a chart and
a color photograph. The designs are very tasteful, but the
charts are small and hard to copy. The cross-stitch designs are mostly worked on linenlike fabric. The projects
include tablecloths, placemats, bell-pulls, pictures, and so
forth. Basic instructions are very brief. The name of the
designer is given for each design.

127 ● Davis, Mary Kay, and Helen Giammattei. Needle-
      point from America's Great Quilt Designs. New
      York: Workman, 1974. 170p. [D]

    Geometric designs are taken from traditional Amer-
ican quilt patterns and transferred to canvas. The authors
use a variety of stitches to produce centered patterns, borders, and continuous designs. Easy-to-follow instructions
show the full design in black-and-white and part of the design on graph paper, making the copying process simple and
easy. Color plates show the finished projects.

128 ● Davis, Mary Kay, and Helen Giammattei. More
      Needlepoint from America's Great Quilt Designs.
      New York: Workman, 1977. 208p. [D]

    Continuing their earlier volume, the authors pre-
sent a wealth of needlepoint patterns based on early American quilts. Each design is illustrated in black-and-white
photographs, with a diagram on the opposite page. Clear
and easy instructions and sixteen pages of full-color photographs of the finished patterns make this book attractive and
useful.

129 ● Davis, Mildred J. Early American Embroidery De-
      signs. New York: Crown, 1969. 159p. [B]

    The book contains about 300 American embroidery

designs from Colonial times to roughly 1825. Photographs
and excellent line drawings accompany each design. The
origins, dates, and present location of the original pieces are
also given. Davis includes clear and easy-to-understand instructions on how to adapt the Colonial designs for modern
use, mostly to clothing, bedspreads, household accessories,
and pictures.

130 ● Davis, Mildred J., ed. Embroidery Designs, 1780-
1820, from the Manuscript Collection, the Textile
Resource and Research Center, the Valentine Museum, Richmond, Virginia. New York: Crown,
1971. 94p. [D]

A collection of designs from the Valentine Museum,
with a short introduction by Davis, consulting curator of the
museum. It includes the designs of the whole notebook by
an unknown author, most probably a woman. The notebook
contains about 300 designs, drawn in ink. The motifs can
be used for many purposes. The distinction of this book is
its rarity. Pattern books dating from 1825 and earlier are
very scarce, and with such extensive coverage as presented
here is almost nonexistent.

131 ● Dawson, Barbara. Metal Thread Embroidery. New
York: Taplinger, 1968. 175p. [C]

Devoted entirely to the techniques and designs appropriate for metal thread. The author discusses every aspect of this kind of work, including its hazards and problems.
The designs are mostly the work of modern artists, and are
shown, unfortunately, mostly in black-and-white photographs.
The book provides inspiration for those who wish to use and
design embroidery using metal threads. Since it is very difficult to work with metal threads, only experienced needleworkers should try this technique.

132 ● Day, F. Lewis, and Mary Buckle. Art Nouveau Embroidery. New York: Sterling, 1974. 262p. [C]

Originally published in 1900, this work is now considered a classic in its field. Using an "artistic" approach,
the authors present many Art Nouveau designs with their
characteristic delicate, curving lines. The purpose of the

designs is not only for copying but as a starting point for
individual creativity. The authors survey the history of embroidery, then proceed to describe many different stitches,
each represented by a project in the Art Nouveau vein. The
illustrations (unfortunately, only in black-and-white) depict
museum pieces or collector's items. Not the usual workbook, but a rich source of inspiration for the experienced.

133 ● Dean, Beryl. Ecclesiastical Embroidery. London:
    Batsford; Newton Centre, Mass.: Branford, 1968
    (© 1958). 258p. [C]

    This illustrated, comprehensive book deals with all
aspects of ecclesiastical embroidery and is not restricted to
any one religion or denomination. The author gives the history of every technique, describing its application through
the centuries. The technical information and instructions
are sufficient, but intended only for the experienced. Not
only a workbook, but a historical essay on needlework used
in different religions.

134 ● Dean, Beryl. Ideas for Church Embroidery. London:
    Batsford; Newton Centre, Mass.: Branford, 1968.
    192p. [C]

    In this volume Dean looks at church embroidery in
a wider perspective. She not only discusses various embroidery projects but includes short articles by other craftspeople, such as architect, silversmith, woodworker, and textile printer. A separate chapter discusses symbolism in
church art and its relevance to needlework in the church.
The greatest value of the book, however, is its presentation
of the projects (mostly modern in form and concept), with
sketches and technical instructions. The projects require
previous experience.

135 ● De Nitto, Elizabeth Brenner. Needlepoint on Plastic
    Canvas. New York: Scribner, 1978. 127p. [C]

    The invention of plastic canvas has added a new
dimension to the world of needlepoint: it is a material that
requires neither blocking nor hemming. The author presents
thirty-four projects in detail, divided into four categories--
home, desk, personal accessories, and gifts. Although the

stitchery is quite simple, the finishing of the products--assembly of the plastic canvas--is not (see, e.g., the handbag). For adventurous needleworkers who like to try something unusual.

136 ● D.M.C. Library. Turkish Embroideries. Edited by
Th. de Dillmont. N.p.: n.p., 1972. 20, 44p.
[C]

Twenty-four color plates with eighty-seven motifs are presented in this book, all borrowed from original Turkish sources. The designs are done in different stitches, mostly embroidery and cross-stitch. Several plates are included with designs ready to trace on paper. The color plates show the actual work. The designs include borders, running patterns, and background designs. The editor gives suggestions for possible uses.

137 ● Donald, Elsie Burch, ed. The Book of Creative
Crafts. London: Octopus, 1978. 256p. [D]

An elegantly produced book with 150 projects, all illustrated in color. The various techniques are discussed in separate chapters: needlepoint, macrame, embroidery, rugmaking, crochet, knitting, and so on. The section on needlepoint presents a nice collection of bargello pillows. The embroidery section shows peasant embroideries from Eastern Europe, drawnwork, a stitch library, and patterns large enough for copying. The other crafts are also sufficiently well covered. The volume can serve both as a workbook and as a reference source.

138 ● Dreesmann, Cecile. Embroidery. New York: Macmillan, 1970. 173p. [A]

This volume is a compact manual for beginners. The author's emphasis is on discovery through experimentation. The content consists of remarks on historical development, fundamental techniques, materials, and tools. One hundred basic stitches are clearly demonstrated with photographs and diagrams. Some of the examples are counted-thread embroidery; others are in the family of crewel embroidery stitches.

139 ● Dreesmann, Cecile. <u>Samplers for Today.</u> New York:
     Galahad, 1972. 160p. [D]

     Originally a means of recording stitches, sampler-
making today serves as both as a storytelling medium and
as a showcase for technical expertise. Samplers gathered
from all over the world are presented in this book, and they
provide countless motifs, techniques, and stitch patterns for
the needleworker. The samplers comprise various subjects,
including numbers and the alphabet, animals, insects, butterflies, maps, coats of arms, flowers, and geometric patterns.
The author provides the user with technical instructions for
the stitches, and she encourages readers to use their own
imagination and creativity. Many photographs of the original
works are included, with a few in color.

140 ● Drooker, Penelope B. <u>Embroidering with the Loom:</u>
     <u>Creative Combinations of Weaving and Stitchery.</u>
     Drawings by Susan Damon Fritz-Herzberg; photo-
     graphs by Jane Lougee Bryant and others. New
     York: Van Nostrand, 1979. 103p. [C]

     In this unusual combination of weaving and stitch-
ery, the author integrates many techniques to achieve unique
effects, as well as save time and effort. Although the techniques involved are quick and simple, the interaction of weaving and embroidery can produce seemingly complex results.
Certain effects are impossible to achieve with either craft
alone. The author presents many applications of these techniques in both traditional and contemporary projects. Photographs (some in color), diagrams of several dozen embroidery stitches, and a large glossary make this book a useful
volume for those who like to try something unusual.

141 ● Drysdale, Rosemary. <u>The Art of Blackwork Embroi-</u>
     <u>dery.</u> New York: Scribner, 1975. 159p. [D]

     In this volume, the author presents a special form
of embroidery popular in medieval and Renaissance England.
Blackwork is a counted-thread embroidery using black yarn
on white fabric. Included in the book are instructions on
stitches, discussion of materials, and a detailed description
of a beginner's project, a pillow. Graphs and good illustrations accompany forty-five patterns. The author presents

twenty projects for needleworkers interested in trying this little-known type of embroidery.

142 ● Drysdale, Rosemary.   Pulled Work on Canvas and
        Linen.   New York: Scribner, 1978.   127p. [C]

    This book attests to the revival of an old technique
that was popular particularly in England and Denmark.   Over
100 stitches are demonstrated, each with diagrams.   The possibilities for combination are almost infinite.   The making
of beautiful lacy patterns can serve as an expression of creative talent.   This is not an easy technique to master; it requires already some experience in traditional needlework.

143 ● Durand, Dianne.   Smocking; Technique, Projects and
        Designs.   New York: Dover, 1979.   56p. [C]

    The art of smocking--a special embroidery tech-
nique--is the subject of this book.   The author provides complete instructions for ten projects: selection of materials,
setting pleats, working smock designs from charts, plus the
basic stitches and their combinations.   Durand explains how
to adapt commercial patterns for smocking and create beautifully decorated garments.   Because of its complicated technique, only needleworkers with previous experience should
attempt this type of embroidery.

144 ● Dyer, Anne, and Valerie Duthoit.   Canvas Work from
        the Start to Finish.   Newton Centre, Mass.:   Bran-
        ford, 1972, 174p. [C]

    Canvaswork, or needlepoint, is the subject of this
book, but the authors go beyond the conventional stitches and
present more complicated combinations that can create specific effects.   Unfortunately, the charts and drawings are not
clear, making their use quite difficult.   Photographs and
drawings are only in black-and-white.   Only very experienced
needleworkers can profit from this book.

145 ● Edmonds, Mary Jaene.   Geometric Designs in Needle-
        point.   New York: Van Nostrand, 1976.   131p. [C]

    Edmonds presents twenty attractive designs that

combine the techniques of needlepoint and bargello. Each
design is accompanied by explicit directions, charts, and
photographs. The last chapter contains an excellent guide
to finishing needlepoint projects. Although the directions
are easy to follow, this technique should only be attempted
by experienced needleworkers. A list of suppliers and some
references are appended.

146 ● Embroidery. Edited by Mary Harding. New York:
Van Nostrand, 1978. 127p. [C]

This book, originally published in Europe, contains mostly English and German patterns. No basic instructions are provided, and consequently it is not suggested
for beginners. The patterns are beautiful, sophisticated,
and colorful. The author divided the book into two sections
--one part, projects for the home; the other, fashion. The
photographs, many of which are in color, are excellent, and
instructions are provided for design.

147 ● Embroidery; A Golden Hands Pattern Book. New
York: Random House, 1973. 128p. [C]

This American publication of an English work contains beautiful patterns and illustrations of finished products.
Measurements and other technical data are included. A glossary of stitches and useful hints complete the book. Since
basic instructions are very brief, this book is not for beginners.

148 ● Embroidery Step-by-Step. New York: Collier, 1976.
64p. [A]

An inexpensive, attractive instruction book, one
volume in Collier's handicraft series. The topic is ap-
proached in an imaginative fashion: a new project in each
chapter introduces the reader to the various tools and materials. The basic stitches are demonstrated through easy-
to-follow instructions and detailed drawings and photographs.
A list of suppliers, in Great Britain and the United States,
and a short bibliography are appended.

149 ● Enthoven, Jacqueline. Stitchery for Children; A Man-

ual for Teachers, Parents and Children.   New
York: Van Nostrand, 1968.   172p. [A]

An interesting and useful manual, mostly for teachers and parents.   The first part covers stages of development in children, specifically their creative ability.   Each
age group is discussed separately, followed by step-by-step
instructions for each stitch.   The next chapter deals with
designing with stitches, inspiring the creative ability of children.   A separate chapter is written for children with special problems, including the mentally retarded.   A useful,
practical manual, serving specific needs.

150 ● Enthoven, Jacqueline.   The Stitches of Creative Em-
      broidery.   New York: Van Nostrand, 1964.   212p.
      [D]

A comprehensive treatment of all aspects of embroidery, presenting more than 200 stitches.   They are clearly described and illustrated in easy-to-follow diagrams.   These
instructions constitute the major part of the book.   The final
section discusses borders; geometric designs; flower, leaf,
and animal forms; and free-hand designs.   Pictures of original works--some historical, some modern--are also presented in the last chapter.

151 ● Epstein, Roslyn.   American Indian Needlepoint De-
      signs for Pillows, Belts, Handbags and Other Pro-
      jects.   New York: Dover, 1973.   48p. [B]

This is not so much a workbook as a collection of
simple American Indian needlepoint designs, suitable for many
applications.   Technical instructions are minimal, but the patterns are worthwhile.   The graphs are clear and easy to follow.

152 ● Fangel, Esther, and others.   Danish Pulled Thread
      Embroidery.   New York: Dover, 1977.   100p. [C]

This book was developed by the members of the
Danish Handworkers Guild.   The first part gives instructions
and diagrams for making forty-five historic designs.   The
second part explains how the designs can be used today to
make various items, such as tablecloths, doilies, and placemats.   Each diagram is accompanied by a photograph of the

finished design. Although instructions are included, pulled-thread embroidery, because of its elaborate and fairly complicated technique, should be attempted only by needleworkers with some experience.

153 ● Farlie, Barbara L., and Constance C. Sloan. Your House in Needlepoint. Needlepoint photographs by Otto Maya; drawings by Sill Weber. Indianapolis: Bobbs-Merrill, 1976. 142p. [C]

The authors of this book teach the readers how to make a needlepoint picture of their homes. After explaining and illustrating all the stitches used in the project, they give the outline and working instructions for a dozen typical houses --Colonial, Tudor, Georgian, contemporary, and so on. Instructions include how to chart and transfer the reader's own design to canvas, and stitches to use for special effects, such as shading of shrubs and brickwork. Experienced needleworkers will be able to create needlework pictures of their homes--more interesting than photographs!

154 ● Farrell, Peg. Counted Cross-Stitch Patchwork Designs. Photographs and graphics by Howard Salten. New York: Van Nostrand, 1980. 127p. [B]

The author takes forty-five of the most popular patchwork (quilt) designs and translates them into cross-stitch. After a short history of quilting and stitchery, she presents the single block patterns, with graphs and photographs of the finished products in color.

155 ● Feiner, Wilhelmina Fox. Adventure in Needlepoint. Garden City, N.Y.: Doubleday, 1973. 116p. [A]

Detailed, expert advice for the beginner on choosing canvas, yarn, and tools. The author is a firm believer in originality and shows how patterns can be created or adapted using a number of different stitches. Instructions are precise and are accompanied by drawings and photographs, some in color.

156 ● Feisner, Edith Anderson. Needlepoint and Beyond: 27 Lessons in Advanced Canvaswork. New York: Scribner, 1980. 175p. [C]

According to the subtitle, this book is not for beginners. The author treats needlepoint as an art, discussing the infinite possibilities of texture, color, shading, and design. The book is unusual in many ways. The twenty-five stitches are divided into four groups--family, coverage, notes, and usage. Instructions are adequate, with clear illustrations, but this is a book only for the experienced.

157 ● Fél, Edit. Hungarian Peasant Embroidery. London: Batsford, 1961. 138p. [C]

A full account of the history, regional characteristics, and techniques of Hungarian peasant embroidery. Different chapters include embroidery on linen, cut-thread work with satin stitch, counted-thread work (cross-stitch), and pulled thread technique. The distinctive embroidery of the furriers (embroidery on lambskin, with the fur inside) is given special consideration. The illustrations are mostly in black-and-white, with a few color plates showing museum pieces. The author discusses the special embroidery techniques of different regions, giving the history and the social place of the craft. Brief technical instructions are included. Although not a workbook, this volume offers beautiful designs that can be used by the experienced needleworker for further applications.

158 ● Felcher, Cecelia. The Needlepoint Workbook of Traditional Designs. New York: Hawthorn, 1973. 233p. [B]

This book contains eighty-seven geometric repeat patterns from African, European, Oriental, and American cultures. They are divided into three areas: border, scatter, and center designs. Graphs and photographs, some in color, show the basic designs. Brief instructions in the basics of needlepoint blocking and finishing are included. The book is a rich inspiration for those who like geometric designs.

159 ● Feldman, Annette. Beginner's Needlecraft. New York: Harper, 1974. 116p. [A]

This practical, handsomely illustrated guide describes eight kinds of needlecraft for the beginner--appliqué,

crewel embroidery, crochet, knitting, rug-hooking, needlepoint, bargello, and patchwork. Each technique is fully detailed and amply illustrated. There are 174 black-and-white
pictures and eight pages of color plates for each craft. A
good, basic guide.

160 ● Fields, Barbara, and Lorelle Phillips. Instant Nee-
        dlepoint Designs. Illustrated by Carol Nicklaus.
        New York: Grosset and Dunlap, 1973. 96p. [A]

    This large-format book enables the reader to copy
the design in its original size directly to the canvas. A
short introduction describes the necessary techniques, stitches,
selection of materials, colors, and so on. The designs are
suggested for various uses, such as pillows, rugs, or wall
hangings. A simple, easy workbook for beginners, although
the more experienced can also use its designs.

161 ● Fischer, Pauline, and Anabel Lasker. Bargello Mag-
        ic; How to Design Your Own. New York: Holt,
        1972. 150p. [B]

    This rich source of beautiful bargello patterns in
color gives detailed instructions for a versatile and no⁻ʸ very
popular technique, known in the past as Irish stitch, flame
stitch, or Hungarian stitch. The authors encourage their
readers to make their own designs on the basis of the samples presented in the book. A separate chapter discusses
border designs. A list of suppliers and a directory of needlework stores round out the volume.

162 ● Fischer, Pauline, and Mary Lou Smith. Egyptian De-
        signs in Modern Stitchery. New York: Dutton,
        1979. 60p. [C]

    The book was inspired by a fascination with the
lore and history of ancient Egypt. The authors adapted twenty-eight Egyptian motifs into modern needlework design.
Each is photographed in full color and reproduced again full-
size in a brown-and-black photo-pattern. The stitches are
either bargello or needlepoint, or variations of these two.
Instructions are given with each design, and each pattern
has a key for the stitches used. New here is the idea of
using canvas as part of the design, which the author devel-

oped especially for this book. Only the more experienced
should attempt these patterns.

163 ● Fisher, Joan. The Creative Art of Needlepoint Tap-
        estry. London and New York: Hamlyn, 1972.
        176p. [C]

      A comprehensive book, presenting every aspect of
needlepoint. After surveying the history of tapestry and needlepoint, the author presents more than twenty projects, with
diagrams, illustrations, and color photographs. A particularly complete dictionary of stitches is included. The designs are both traditional and modern, and the author encourages users to create their own designs as well.

164 ● Fisher, Joan. Joan Fisher's Guide to Embroidery.
        London: Triune, 1973. 144p. [D]

      The term "embroidery" in this book also embraces
needlepoint, smocking, patchwork, appliqué, and quilting. A
chapter is devoted to each technique, giving clear instructions. A project, representing each type of needlework, is
presented with charts and color photographs. A rich collection of many projects, this is also a good workbook for both
beginners and the more experienced.

165 ● Fisher, Joan. Joan Fisher's Guide to Needlecraft.
        London: Triune, 1972. 144p. [B]

      This book provides an introduction to seven basic
needlecraft techniques--knitting, crochet, embroidery, needlepoint, tapestry, macrame, and sewing. Directions for
the stitches and techniques for each craft are fully illustrated with clear diagrams, sketches, and photographs (some in
color). Whether readers are interested in only one craft or
in all, they will find precise instructions. Although the author states that the book is useful for both beginners and the
experienced, most of the projects require some previous experience with the craft.

166 ● Fontana, Frank. Patchwork Quilt Designs for Needle-
        point, Charted for Easy Use. New York: Dover,
        1976. 42p. [B]

Fontana, a graphic artist, found that the geometric designs of antique quilts adapted beautifully to needlepoint. He charted several of them, and the result is this book. He sees these patchwork quilt designs lending themselves most readily to pillows. Some interesting color combinations are suggested by the illustrations on the front and back covers. Information about the quilts' history is included with each design. The introduction describes the various stitches.

167 ● Foris, Maria, and Andreas Foris. Charted Folk Designs for Cross-Stitch Embroidery. (Original title: Susann Folk Cross-Stitch Charts.) New York: Dover, 1975. 77p. [D]

A rich collection of ancient folk embroideries from the countries along the Danube. Some 278 charts in two colors (black and red on white background) represent a great variety of patterns: tulip, onion, rose, peacock, and so on. Geometric designs and running and corner patterns are also included. The charts are most appropriate for cross-stitch, but might be adapted to needlepoint or rug-hooking. Not a how-to book, but a great collection of designs.

168 ● Francini, Audrey A. Crewel Embroidery with Texture and Thread Variations. New York: Van Nostrand, 1979. 152p. [D]

The author describes the various embroidery stitches with careful instructions and clear, easy-to-follow illustrations. The designs progress from the simple to the more complicated. Color pictures of some of the finished projects, and black-and-white drawings for the patterns (with color key), are included. A useful workbook, containing a rich collection of embroidery designs.

169 ● Fraser, B. Kay. Modern Stitchery; Stitches, Patterns, Free-Form Designing. New York: Crown, 1976. 108p. [C]

A modern application of crewel and other embroidery stitches for decorating the home and making accessories (clothing included). After giving technical instructions, the author presents many projects with drawings and photographs,

some in color. The designs are mostly bright in hue and
try to use the various stitches in an original way. Since
some of the designs are elaborate, their execution requires
some previous experience.

170 ● Gaber, Susan. A Treasury of Flower Designs for
    Artists, Embroiderers, and Craftsmen. New York:
    Dover, 1981. 80p. [C]

    Artistic yet botanically accurate line drawings of
a great variety of flowers are presented in this book: zinnia,
pansy, aster, lilac, petunia, rose, tulip, and many others.
Some 150 illustrations, ready to be used by embroiderers or
craftsmen, make for a rich collection of floral patterns.

171 ● Gartner, Louis J. Needlepoint Design. New York:
    Morrow, 1970. 191p. [C]

    This book was written to teach users how to cre-
ate original designs and transfer them to canvas. The technical instructions are detailed and clear, but the most original part of the book is Gartner's own designs. Over 100
patterns can be copied or adapted from the book; forty are
shown in finished form, on color plates. Using the two basic needlepoint stitches (continental and basket weave), the
author shows great versatility in his designs.

172 ● Gartner, Louis J. More Needlepoint Design. New
    York: Morrow, 1975. 192p. [C]

    Following the style and format of his earlier vol-
ume, Gartner presents in this book another collection of his
original designs. Basic instructions are kept to a minimum,
and the designs are grouped according to their use, or distinctive type, such as chair seats, animal designs, and rug
patterns. The designs can be copied from the book or used
as a basis for further individual design.

173 ● Geddes, Elizabeth, and Moyra McNeill. Blackwork
    Embroidery. New York: Dover, 1976. 115p. [C]

    Blackwork is a form of counted-thread embroidery
that uses a single color of thread (black) in different textures,

and employs various embroidery stitches. After surveying
the history of the craft, the author covers contemporary
techniques, materials, threads, and how to make a design.
Some 200 illustrations are presented in the book, including
border patterns, birds, animals, and fruits. This volume
is not for beginners, since blackwork requires some previous experience in embroidery. A list of American suppliers is appended.

174 ● Gentles, Margaret. Turkish and Greek Island Em-
        broideries; From the Burton Yost Berry Collec-
        tion in the Art Institute of Chicago. Chicago:
        Art Institute of Chicago, 1964. 53p. [C]

        This book contains fifty-three color photographs of
masterpieces from that part of the Mediterranean. The
pieces are mostly from the sixteenth to the nineteenth centuries. In the introduction, the author discusses the origin,
development, and importance of needlework in the life of
the people. The technique, shown on the plates, is embroidery, using many stitches, colors, and materials. This is
not a workbook, but a beautiful collection of needleworks,
elevated by the simple peasants of the area to the level of
art.

175 ● Gibbon, M. A. Canvas Work; A Practical Guide.
        London: Bell, 1965. 95p. [D]

        This basic workbook presents a dictionary of
stitches, with clear, easy-to-follow instructions and graphs.
The author includes all the necessary practical hints, and
the projects are illustrated with photographs (unfortunately,
in black-and-white). The designs can be used by both beginners and more experienced needleworkers.

176 ● Gilberg, Laura J., and Barbara Ballinger Buchholz.
        Needlepoint Designs from Amish Quilts. New
        York: Scribner, 1977. 143p. [D]

        Twenty-seven geometrical designs are presented
in this book, derived from quilts made by the Amish of
eastern Pennsylvania, Ohio, Indiana, and Kansas. Quilt
patterns adapt very well to needlepoint. Since each design
is a square, the worker is not limited to pillows, because

the squares can be multiplied and used for other purposes, mostly for rugs. The patterns are well illustrated with diagrams, color charts, and photographs. They should appeal to those who like unusual geometric designs.

177 ● Gilmore, Betty. The Needlepoint Primer. New York: Chilton, 1973. 146p. [A]

Addressed to the beginner, this primer offers easy-to-follow instructions for a variety of needlepoint projects, starting with a simple napkin ring and progressing to increasingly complex pieces. Illustrations include clear diagrams, black-and-white photographs, and a few color plates demonstrating the completed work. A brief list of suppliers in Europe, Mexico, and the United States is appended.

178 ● Gladstone, Meredith. Small Needlepoint Treasures: A Complete How-to Workbook for Making Quick Needlepoint Gifts. New York: Morrow, 1979. 128p. [B]

According to the author, needlepoint projects should not take forever to complete. To prove this point, she presents Victorian-inspired small projects for framing, matting, covering bookends, and so forth. The area to cover is on the average smaller than usual and faster to finish. Instructions are good, and designs are clear and easy to copy. The lack of interior photographs can serve as an impetus to creativity.

179 ● Gladstone, Meredith, and Gary Gladstone. The Needle-point ALPHABET Book. New York: Morrow, 1973. 183p. [B]

The Gladstones concentrate on the wealth of design ideas to be found in typography and alphabets, offering many photographs, charts, and easy-to-follow directions. The material includes three samplers and twenty-two complete alphabets. The projects comprise not only the traditional pillows but purses, hats, blouses, rugs, and boxes. Stitches are mostly in needlepoint, but some projects are in bargello (flame) stitch.

180 ● Goble, Dora Ann. Needlepoint Insignia of the Armed

Forces; Including Instructions for Cross-Stitch and Latch-Hook. New York: Van Nostrand, 1978. 160p. [C]

This unique pattern book contains 125 graphed emblems and insignia of the U. S. Armed Forces. Each can either be worked in needlepoint or made into a rug or wall hanging with latch-hook. The graphs are color-coded and the author gives general instructions for working techniques, blocking, and finishing. A unique collection of patterns, for the more experienced. An index of the emblems is included.

181 ● Godey's Lady's Book. Victorian Needlepoint Designs from Godey's Lady's Book and Peterson's Magazine. Edited by Rita Weiss. New York: Dover, 1976. 48p. [C]

Unusual needlepoint designs from two Victorian women's magazines, charted for easy use. Forty-three designs are presented in this book, including flowers, animals, dancers, and river-and-bridge scenes. Since some of the designs are quite elaborate, and instructions are very basic, this is only for the more experienced needleworker.

182 ● Goldman, Sylvia. The Art of Needlegraph. Secaucus, N. J.: Derby, 1974. 128p. [D]

Forty-five original needlepoint designs, each reproduced in full color. Needlegraph is provided for each design at the facing page with step-by-step instructions. The book is divided into easy, intermediate, and advanced designs and offers a wide range of colors, sizes, and styles to choose from. The instructions give detailed information on how to select and prepare materials, transfer the graph to canvas, determine size of stitches, and finish the project.

183 ● Goodman, Frances Schaill. The Embroidery of Mexico and Guatemala. New York: Scribner, 1976. 81p. [C]

This is not the usual how-to book. The author traces the history of embroidery in two Latin American countries and analyzes the various stitches and techniques. She discusses the development of native embroidery, how it is related to different fabrics, and how it is used in native gar-

ments. The designs can serve as inspiration for the modern
embroiderer, since the excellent color pictures could be
copied and adapted for modern use.

184 ● Gorham, Georgia L., and Jeanne M. Warth. A Treas-
      ury of Charted Designs for Needleworkers. New
      York: Dover, 1977. 48p. [B]

    The author presents 141 charted designs, including
a great variety of patterns, such as owl, flamingo, cat, piano,
spinning wheel. Each design has a suggested color key, and
each is worked on an easy-to-read grid. Since basic instructions are kept to a minimum, some experience is needed to execute the designs.

185 ● Gostelow, Mary. Blackwork. New York: Van No-
      strand, 1976. 160p. [D]

    Gostelow describes the origin, development, and
various styles of this type of embroidery. Blackwork is
worked with black thread on white material. It became popular in England during the Tudor period. From England,
it spread to the United States and other countries. Holbein's
influence on blackwork styles is discussed in a chapter on
artistic blackwork, and it is considered in relation to period
costume. The last chapter, "Useful Blackwork," discusses
modern applications. Richly illustrated with color plates
(mostly from museums and art galleries), black-and-white
pictures, and drawings, this book contains no patterns, although basic instructions, stitches, and necessary supplies
are covered.

186 ● Gostelow, Mary. Embroidery of All Russia. New
      York: Scribner, 1977. 158p. [C]

    A rich collection of Russian folk art (several items
are museum pieces), worked with various stitches--e.g.,
cross-stitch, needlepoint, and embroidery. Included are
many color plates and easy-to-follow charts for certain decorative elements applicable to many projects.

187 ● Gostelow, Mary. Embroidery South Africa. New
      York: Transatlantic Arts, 1977. 104p. [D]

Many types of embroidery are discussed in this volume, although they are not specifically South African. The only "real South African" contribution to the book is the discussion of the Voortrekker tapestry, a rival to the Bayeux. The bibliography lists sources for further information regarding that particular tapestry.

188 ● Grafton, Carol Belanger. Geometric Needlepoint Designs. New York: Dover, 1975. 48p. [B]

This book contains forty-three imaginative geometric designs, inspired by the current interest in abstract art. When the projects are completed, many of the designs will appear as three-dimensional, or as op art. They are adaptable to many projects, such as pillows, belts, purses, and wall hangings. Twenty-two designs are presented in full color on the covers.

189 ● Gray, Jennifer. Canvas Work. Newton Centre, Mass.: Branford, 1974. 128p. [B]

This book presents an assortment of attractive designs suitable for needlepoint (canvaswork). Technical instructions are sufficient and easy to follow, accompanied by photographs of the finished products (some in color). A good workbook, suitable for the beginner or intermediate level.

190 ● Grier, Rosey. Rosey Grier's Needlepoint for Men. New York: Walker, 1973. 158p. [C]

The author, a former football player, here tackles his hobby, needlepoint. He displays his own designs, which are, in his opinion, masculine. The projects are arranged by purpose--for yourself, for the home, for sports items, and so on. Among his designs are many interesting and original patterns. Unfortunately, the patterns are not shown on graph paper and so are impossible to copy. However, Grier does present certain motifs on graphs, such as letters of the alphabet, flags, and card suits. The last chapter discusses and shows the works of other men who have selected needlepoint as their hobby. He gives the reader some technical instructions, mostly to those who attempt to design their own. An interesting book--not the usual how-to approach--that offers beautiful designs and encourages users to rely on their creative ability.

191 ● Gross, Judith. Needlepoint Designs for Chair Covers. New York: Van Nostrand, 1979. 128p. [D]

Thirty beautiful chair-cover designs for needlepoint are presented in this volume, ranging from Oriental to specifically modern motifs. A graph outline (very easy to copy onto mono canvas) and color chart are included with each design. The photographs of the finished products are shown in full color. An attractive and inspiring workbook for anyone who wants to transform an old chair into an heirloom.

192 ● Gross, Nancy D., and Frank Fontana. Shisha Embroidery. New York: Dover, 1981. 80p. [C]

Shisha embroidery, or the technique of working tiny decorative mirrors into fabric, is a venerable art throughout western India, Pakistan, Baluchistan, and Afghanistan. This book presents a short history of this unique art and describes its techniques. Complete instructions, with illustrated stitches, enable needleworkers to stitch the mirrors according to the patterns, or as their imagination suggests. The patterns are all adapted from actual Indian artifacts shown in full color on the covers. A list of supply sources for authentic Indian mirrors is provided.

193 ● Grow, Judith. Classic Needlework: Contemporary Designs Inspired by the American Past. Photographs by Kenneth Kaplowitz. New York: Van Nostrand, 1976. 112p. [C]

Following a brief history of American needlework, the author presents a comprehensive chapter on the basics: tools, needles, frames, hoops, and other supplies, and the preferred materials for both free and counted-thread embroidery. Thirty stitches are described in detail. Grow took her designs from the American past, from crewel bedspreads to Talish rugs. The last chapter of the book shows the original pieces and the contemporary projects, and makes suggestions for further use.

194 ● Grow, Judith K., and Elizabeth C. McGrail. Creating

Historic Samplers.   Princeton, N.J.:   Pyne, 1974.
127p. [B]

    After an introductory chapter on the history of
American samplers, the authors present detailed instructions
on how to create a historic sampler today.   They describe
materials and stitches and offer a number of charts with different motifs, such as alphabets, numbers, flowers, borders,
birds, and human figures.   Many photographs of original
samplers, from museums or private collections, are shown.
Unfortunately, very few are in color.   A useful book for
those who would like to create a sampler based on original,
historic designs.

195 ● Guild, Vera P.   Creative Use of Stitches.   Rev. ed.
        Worcester, Mass.:   Davis, 1971 © 1969).   64p.
        [C]

    After explaining and illustrating the basic stitches
of embroidery, the author presents the artistic works of
modern embroiderers, partially in color, but mostly in
black-and-white pictures.

196 ● Gullers, Barbara Donnelly.   The Crewel Needlepoint
        World.   New York: Van Nostrand, 1973.   112p.
        [B]

    Produced by a Scandinavian needleworker, this
book has a somewhat misleading title, since it includes both
crewel embroidery and needlepoint.   The common denomina-
tor of both techniques is that both are worked in wool.   Besides the basic instructions, different stitches are presented,
and their practical use is illustrated with various projects.
The wealth of color photographs, showing both finished projects and stitches, makes this book attractive and easy to
use.

197 ● Hall, Nancy, and Jean Riley.   Bargello Borders.   New
        York: Scribner, 1977.   159p. [C]

    This is a rich collection of bargello patterns (also
called Florentine stitch or Hungarian stitch), adapted for borders or frames.   However, as the authors point out, the
designs can also be used as continuous patterns for pillows,
wall hangings, and other items.   The book contains clear

technical instructions, charts, drawings, and color illustrations. A good workbook, suitable for intermediate or advanced students.

198 ● Halpern, Frieda. Full-Color Russian Folk Needlepoint Designs. New York: Dover, 1980. 32p. [B]

The book contains thirty-one full-page designs in color, adapted from Russian folk art. Riders on horseback, flowers, birds, mythical beasts, and geometric designs are among the many patterns. All are adapted for use on #10 mono canvas, for needlepoint, cross-stitch, or rug-hooking. Since instructions are basic, some experience is needed for the use of this book.

199 ● Hanley, Hope. The Craft of Needlepoint; 101 Stitches and How to Use Them. New York: Scribner, 1977. 112p. [A]

This basic book of stitches, intended for the beginner, offers clear directions, with drawings and charts. No projects are presented here, but anyone who needs instruction or clarification in the bewildering variety of needlepoint stitches can find examples in this book.

200 ● Hanley, Hope. Fun with Needlepoint. New York: Scribner, 1972. 95p. [A]

Instructions for the beginner who wants to learn to make simple items using needlepoint. Hanley's descriptions include three types of basic needlepoint stitch (continental, plain half-cross, and basket weave). She gives suggestions for making fifteen articles, such as pin-cushions, belts, and paperweights. Illustrated with photographs (some in color) and drawings. A good starting book for young people, but adults can benefit from it, too.

201 ● Hanley, Hope. Hope Hanley's Patterns for Needlepoint. New York: Scribner, 1976. 110p. [C]

Directed to the intermediate or experienced needleworker, this is, in the author's words a "mix-and-match book." The usual instructions about materials, color, yarn finishing, and so forth are not included. Instead, the user is free to experiment with any of these elements. The book contains seventy-nine designs with a graph and color photograph of the finished piece. There are a few sentences on the design's source, how it can be used, and some working hints. The patterns are geometric, or incorporate the letters of the alphabet. The last chapter describes eleven stitches.

202 ● Hanley, Hope. Needlepoint. Rev. and enl. ed. New York: Scribner, 1975. 175p. [D]

A classic guide for beginners and advanced needleworkers, substantially revised and enlarged since the first edition of 1969. The author discusses every practical question connected with needlepoint. Over eighty stitches are shown with step-by-step illustrations and a photograph of the finished stitch. Hanley also indicates whether a mono, two-thread, or interlock canvas is best for the project. Black-and-white, and some color, photographs of historical and modern needlework illustrate the book.

203 ● Hanley, Hope. Needlepoint in America. New York: Scribner, 1969. 160p. [C]

In this book, Hanley surveys the history of American needlepoint. She searched old needlework and pattern books, newspaper announcements and advertisements, magazines, and old books for information on European origins of American needlepoint. Several old stitches are explained and diagrammed for modern use and easy adaptation. Chapters on the technical aspects of needlepoint explain the stitches and materials and supply all the necessary information for finishing a project.

204 ● Hanley, Hope. Needlepoint Rugs. New York: Scribner, 1971. 115p. [C]

A dependable guide to basic steps and creative designs. The author discusses sources of designs; selection of rug canvas and yarns; techniques for joining rugs; methods of putting designs on canvas; and blocking, edging, and other finishing touches. The stitches and patterns are excellently diagrammed with color plates and black-and-white photographs.

The book is a rich source of contemporary and traditional needlepoint rug designs.

205 ● Hanley, Hope. Needlework Styles for Period Furniture. New York: Scribner, 1978. 176p. [B]

Hanley goes beyond her well-established reputation as a designer of needlework and combines in this volume the history of furniture with needlework styles. She covers the style of different periods with text, photographs (some in color), line drawings, and a list of motifs for needlepoint embroidery. The book is suitable for the intermediate level, not for beginners.

206 ● Hanley, Hope. New Methods in Needlepoint. New York: Scribner, 1966. 96p. [C]

Hanley, author of many needlepoint books, presents in this volume a new technique, the binding stitch. Her purpose is to give professional finish to the projects and to speed up and simplify the making of many articles. The book contains thirteen projects, illustrated with diagrams and photographs. The stitches needed for the various projects are not new, but the finishing instructions offer new methods for experienced needleworkers.

207 ● Hansen, Edith, and Ingrid Hansen. Counted Thread Embroidery. New York: Van Nostrand, 1968. 76p. [B]

This book was originally published in Denmark: counted-thread embroidery is very popular in the Scandinavian countries. Using both traditional and original motifs the authors have produced beautiful designs for such items as embroidered boxes, mirror frames, handbags, and tablecloths. They stress the importance of using the right materials to obtain the maximum effect. Large, clear diagrams show every stitch, and photographs of the finished articles are included. Once the stitches have been mastered, users can make up their own designs for decorating with embroidery.

208 ● Haraszty, Eszter, and Bruce David Colen. Needle-

painting; A Garden of Stitches.   New York: Live-
right, 1974.   114p. [D]

In what is much more than a beautiful how-to book,
the authors present a unique embroidery style, called needle-
painting, which they use to make flowers--"to cultivate an
indoor garden with stitches and brilliant yarns." They present complete and easy-to-understand instructions, with sixty-
one color plates and many black-and-white pictures. This
book should help the user to create imaginative embroidery
projects based on the authors' original patterns.

209 ● Harayda, Marel.   Needlework Magic with Two Basic
        Stitches: Young Ideas for Canvas and Yarn.
        New York: McKay, 1978.   114p. [A]

Harayda, a teacher of needlecraft to children, presents two simple needlepoint stitches--Gobelin and continental
--for young people.   She applies them to numerous simple
projects and discusses the basic materials needed.   The projects are divided into two categories: woven canvas and
plastic canvas.   Guidelines for finishing techniques are provided.   A list of mail-order sources and a metric-equivalent
chart are appended.

210 ● Haupt-Battaglia, Heidi.   Practical Embroidery.   I.
        Mats, Clothes and Runners.   Newton Centre, Mass.:
        Branford, 1968.   166p. [C]

A collection of over seventy designs prepared by
the author.   The designs are varied in patterns, stitches,
colors, materials, and motifs.   The technique is mostly embroidery (various stitches), with a few cross-stitch applications.
The designs are often intricate and demanding, requiring
some experience.   They are fully described and illustrated
with photographs, some in color.   A good workbook.

211 ● Hauschild, Jana.   Danish Cross-Stitch Zodiac Sam-
        plers.   New York: Dover, 1980.   54p. [B]

Twelve elegant samplers are presented here by a
creative Danish designer.   Each sampler is based on one of
the twelve signs of the Zodiac.   The symbol is the starting
point for a wide variety of motifs that are virtually inter-

changeable: flowers, borders, alphabets, butterflies, birds, and so on. The charts are clear and easy to follow. Color reproductions of the finished projects are shown on the inside of the covers. Requiring a little experience, the designs can be adapted for needlepoint or latch-hook.

212 ● Hedin, Solweig, and Jo Springer. Creative Needle-
        work. Photographs by Frank Stork. New York:
        Arco, 1969. 128p. [A]

The authors offer illustrated, step-by-step directions for a dozen needlework techniques, including cross-stitch, crewel, embroidery, Hardanger, appliqué, and needlepoint. They provide good basic instructions with simple projects to introduce the novice to the various techniques. Black-and-white charts, and color pictures of the finished projects, are included. A useful book for beginners.

213 ● Hein, Gisela. Basic Stitches of Embroidery; A Mod-
        ern Approach. New York: Van Nostrand, 1971.
        79p. (Translation of the German original, pub-
        lished in 1969.) [C]

A modern application of embroidery stitches, presenting unusual patterns, reminiscent of or influenced by modern Swedish stitchery. No specific projects are presented--only the stitches, techniques, and possible applications. For those who already have some experience in embroidery and prefer modern to traditional patterns.

214 ● Hines, Millie. American Heirloom Bargello: Designs
        from Quilts, Coverlets, and Navaho Rugs. New
        York: Crown, 1977. 80p. [A]

The author borrows the patterns of Navaho rugs and early American quilts and adapts them to bargello form. Twenty-four designs are presented with graphs, color photographs, yarn colors, and working instructions. Since bargello is a simple stitch, it is suitable for beginners, although the book gives no indication of the quantity of yarns required, a gap that can cause confusion for beginners.

215 ● Hodgson, Mary Anne, and Josephine Ruth Paine. Fast

and Easy Needlepoint.   Garden City, N.Y.:   Doubleday, 1978.   96p. [A]

This workbook for young people begins with a shop-
ping list for basic, inexpensive materials and follows with
seven colorful learning designs.   Each design introduces a
new needlepoint stitch.   Illustrations for the stitches are
clear and easy to follow.   After the technical details, the
authors discuss finishing, blocking, and mounting of needlepoint projects.   The directions are illustrated with drawings,
photographs, and stitch charts.   All designs have been created especially for beginners.   Illustrations are only in black-
and-white.

216 ● Holz, Loretta.   Teach Yourself Stitchery.   New York:
        Lothrop, 1974.   160p. [A]

This book describes some fifteen useful stitches
and suggests projects on which to try them.   Clear diagrams
of the stitches and designs are helpful.   However, the black-
and-white photographs of the completed works are sometimes
too poor for one to discern details.   A chapter on embroidery history, a section on designing projects, and a list of
United States suppliers make this book a useful guide for
young people or those just starting the art of needlework.

217 ● Houck, Carter.   White Work.   New York: Dover,
        1977.   64p. [C]

This volume contains 188 designs from an early
twentieth-century catalog published by the Johann Merken-
thaler factory in Nuremberg.   It deals with whitework, an
old embroidery technique that is once again becoming popular.   Since it employs white thread on white fabric, the
beauty of the finished product depends upon the excellence
of the embroiderer's skill.   A separate chapter explains sixteen stitches for whitework and is followed by a brief discussion of the history of the craft.   A useful volume.

218 ● Houck, Carter, and Myron Miller.   The Boat Buff's
        Book of Embroidery; Needlepoint--Crewel--Appli-
        qué.   New York: Scribner, 1979.   90p. [B]

For boat lovers, the authors present nearly fifty

ideas for projects to make with nautical motifs, including
rugs, pillows, duffelbags, totes, pictures, and ornaments
for clothing.   After an introduction on materials and techniques, the projects are described using one of the three
techniques listed in the title.   Every design is illustrated
with charts, drawings, and color photographs.   A collection
of nautical designs rarely found in other volumes.

219 ● Howard, Constance.   Embroidery and Colour.   New
       York: Van Nostrand, 1976.   216p. [C]

       The emphasis of this book is not on the technical
aspects of embroidery but rather on the use and application
of color in various projects.   Individual sections of the book
consider color and symbol, color mixing, color principles,
and so on.   The text is illustrated with drawings, photographs, and sixty-two color plates.   The author also describes many embroidery techniques, with special reference
to color combinations.

220 ● Howe, Margery Burnham.   Deerfield Embroidery.
       New York: Scribner, 1976.   240p. [C]

       Howe details the history of the Massachusetts town
up to 1890 and describes the formation of the Deerfield Society of Blue and White Needlework.   The characters and
artistic contributions of the seven eighteenth-century women
whose works were used as reference by the Deerfield Society
are closely examined.   In the final section, the author explains how to work the twenty-one Deerfield embroidery
stitches and discusses the necessary equipment and materials.   Illustrations display the patterns in full size, sometimes in black-and-white or in color, but mostly in blue-
and-white, according to the color scheme of this particular
embroidery.

221 ● Hughes, Therle.   English Domestic Needlework, 1660-
       1860.   London: Abbey Fine Arts, 196?   255p.

       After presenting a general history, the author dis-
cusses each type of embroidery in its own chapter, placing
each technique in historical context.   The book contains forty-
eight black-and-white illustrations and four color plates, mostly items from museums and private collections.   This is not

a workbook but is intended for those "who look at embroideries, rather than those who make them." A very thorough
historical treatment of all types of English embroideries.

222 ● Huish, Marcus. Samplers and Tapestry Embroideries.
2nd ed. New York: Dover, 1979. 176p. [C]

This book covers more than two centuries of samplers, mostly of American and British origin, including popular designs, stitches, inscriptions, and much social lore.
It contains twenty-four plates, eight in color. The designs
can easily be adapted to needlepoint, cross-stitch, or latch-
hook. Since basic instructions are not included, this volume
is for the skilled needleworker or for the collector.

223 ● Hurlburt, Regina. Left-handed Needlepoint. Drawings by Robin Hall. New York: Van Nostrand,
1972. 64p. [D]

The author describes and illustrates the various
needlepoint stitches, adapted for left-handed people. No
projects are presented here, only the stitches, with drawings, charts, and enlarged photos of each stitch. A helpful book for left-handers who are frustrated with the countless needlepoint books made only for right-handed people.

224 ● Iglehart, Susan, and Barbara Schweizer. The Quickpoint Book. New York: Holt, 1977. 104p. [A]

Intended for beginners, this book offers a wealth
of information about quickpoint--large stitches using #5 mono
canvas. After all the necessary technical information, the
authors present projects especially suitable for quickpoint,
such as handbags, pillows, pin-cushions, tennis-racquet covers, and carryall bags. The stitches and the patterns are
demonstrated with graphs and drawings; the finished projects
are shown in color photographs.

225 ● Ireys, Katherine. Finishing and Mounting Your Needlepoint Pieces. New York: Crowell, 1973. 232p.
[C]

This book contains not only instructions for finish-

ing and mounting needlepoint pieces but gives detailed descriptions of over forty needlepoint projects, such as pillows,
belts, handbags, and neckties. However, the emphasis is on
the finishing touches; blocking, lining, mitering corners, and
so on. The reader can also find complete information on
how to make trims of braid, cord, fringe, and tassels. The
text is illustrated with many drawings and sketches. A practical, useful volume for every needleworker.

226 ● Irvine, Elizabeth. Classic Posters for Needlepoint.
        New York: Dover, 1980. 48p. [C]

        This book contains twenty-seven famous posters by
such artists as Mucha, the Beggarstaffs, and Will Bradley.
All are charted for needlepoint, counted cross-stitch, or
latch-hook. The designs can be adapted to make pillows,
wall hangings, and other items. Yarn and canvas requirements and suggested color schemes are given for each design. Not a how-to book, this volume does contain unusual
patterns for the more experienced.

227 ● Jarry, Madeleine, and Maryvonne Dobry. Period Nee-
        dlepoint for Antique Furniture. Translated by Phyl-
        lis Freeman. New York: Morrow, 1976. 127p.
        [C]

        The French authors discuss the elegant pastime of
French ladies: petit-point and needlepoint. They survey the
history of needlepoint and tapestry in France and translate
eighteen exquisite seventeenth- and eighteenth-century designs
into needlework patterns for contemporary use. Richly illustrated with black-and-white and some color photographs, the
book could be a source of inspiration to develop further variations and adapt them for various projects. Suitable only
for the experienced needleworker.

228 ● Jessen, Ellen. Ancient Peruvian Textile Design in
        Modern Stitchery. New York: Van Nostrand, 1972.
        64p. [B]

        Designs based on ancient Peruvian textiles are pre-
sented in this book, suitable for cross-stitch, needlepoint,
and--in a few cases--embroidery. After a brief introduction
to the history of Peruvian culture in general, and textiles in

particular, Jessen presents a rich collection of motifs, suitable for different projects. Several finished articles are represented in full color photographs. The author also gives suggestions for further application of the different designs.

229 ● Johansson, Barbara. Favorite Pets in Charted Designs. New York: Dover, 1979. 32p. [B]

This book contains twenty-two charted designs of pets--puppies, kittens, rabbits, canaries, parakeets, and so on. These designs can be worked in many techniques, but primarily in needlepoint, counted cross-stitch, or latch-hook. Each design has its own color key, and the finished products in full color are presented on the covers. Simple basic instructions are included in the introduction. Not a how-to book, but rather a collection of designs ready to be used for various techniques, or according to the ideas of the user.

230 ● John, Edith. Needleweaving. Newton Centre, Mass.; Branford, 1970. 88p. [D]

John concentrates on the ancient art of needleweaving, as seen in Coptic, Norwegian, Turkish, and other museum pieces and adapted to modern taste through a variation of stitching techniques. The book gives guidance to experienced and also beginning needleworkers, presenting clear diagrams and excellent photographs, some showing the author's own work. Choice of fabric, thread, and color is also discussed. Suggestions are made for domestic, church, and costume ornamentation.

231 ● Johnson, Mary Elizabeth. Pillows: Designs, Patterns, Projects. Birmingham, Ala.: Oxmoor, 1978. 192p. [D]

Forty-four designs are presented here for pillows of all kinds and shapes. Different needlework techniques are covered, including needlepoint, bargello, and embroidery. The book has good illustrations and general instructions on working from a charted design, enlarging patterns, and finishing the project.

232 ● Jones, Mary Eirwen. A History of Western Embroidery. New York: Watson-Guptill, 1969. 159p. [C]

The emphasis of this book is not on technical know-how but on the history and development of embroidery from medieval through modern times. Illustrations (some in color) are presented from various European countries; one chapter discusses embroidery in America. This work is for readers interested in the historical and cultural background of embroidery. A list of relevant British and American museums and a short bibliography are appended.

233 ● Justema, William, and Doris Justema. Weaving and Needlecraft Color Course. New York: Van Nostrand, 1971. 160p. [C]

This book is a unique guide, prepared specifically for those who work with thread. The authors, a weaver and a designer, felt the need for such a book throughout their professional careers. The book is divided into two parts. The first discusses color theories; the second is the heart of the book. Ten types of color schemes are explained, and for each one five widely varied projects are presented--fifty projects in all. A glossary of terms, a bibliography, and an index add to the usefulness of the book, which is not the usual how-to book, but literally a "course in color" with applications in the field of weaving and needlecrafts.

234 ● Kaestner, Dorothy. Bargello Antics. Photographs by George Kaestner. New York: Scribner, 1979. 79p. [B]

Bargello enthusiasts will be delighted with this book. It presents a beautiful collection of four-way and regular bargello patterns. Kaestner gives clear instructions, and her charts are easy to follow. Each design is color-coded, and the finished products are illustrated in full color. The author also suggests creative variations that can be made from the basic patterns. Since it includes only minimal instructions, this book should be used by the more experienced.

235 ● Kaestner, Dorothy. Designs for Needlepoint and Latch-Hook Rugs. Photographs by George Kaestner. New York: Scribner, 1978. 177p. [C]

A beautiful collection of twenty-five rug patterns for various sizes and shapes. The designs are mostly Oriental, with a few in modern and traditional style. After short technical instructions, the designs are described and illustrated with charts on graph paper, color key included. Since the Oriental patterns are very intricate, this volume is suitable only for the more experienced needleworker.

236 ● Kaestner, Dorothy. Four Way Bargello. Rev. ed. Photographs by George Kaestner. New York: Scribner, 1974. 117p. [B]

A novel application of the bargello stitch is presented here. Instead of working in parallel lines, the needleworker works out from the center, and makes kaleidoscopic patterns. The book contains a large collection of these patterns, using either contrasting or gradating colors. Working instructions are given, together with illustrations, many in color. Anyone who has mastered regular bargello can progress to these four-way designs and enjoy the challange that they offer.

237 ● Kaestner, Dorothy. Needlepoint Bargello. Photographs by George Kaestner. New York: Scribner, 1974. 136p. [B]

Following the methods of her earlier book, Four Way Bargello, Kaestner presents in this book twenty-five entirely new four-way bargello patterns. Each is accompanied by a chart for working and a color picture of the finished piece. The book also includes thirty-two regular bargello patterns suitable for needlepoint stitch, and one pattern combining the two methods. A very useful book with ready-made patterns, this volume could also serve as a source for further experimentation and individual design.

238 ● Kalina, Judith Schoener. Bible Stitchery. New York: Doubleday, 1980. 100p. [D]

Forty projects are presented in this book, interpretations of famous passages from both the Old and New Testaments. They comprise simple and more complicated projects, suitable for both beginners and more experienced. The projects include graphs, with yarn colors, suggested stitches, and many possibilities for individual creativity. The usual instructions on materials and methods are included and also color plates of the finished projects.

239 ● Kassell, Hilda. Stitches in Time; The Art and History of Embroidery. New York: Duell, 1966. 108p. [D]

The author traces the history of our country through the illustrated stories that were embroidered on samplers, from Colonial days to modern times. The second part of the book contains technical directions and a well-illustrated dictionary of stitches. An unusual collection of American samplers, serving either as a model to be copied, or giving inspirations for individual design. The techniques are embroidery and cross-stitch, suitable for both beginners and more experienced needleworkers.

240 ● Katzenberg, Gloria. Needlepoint and Patterns, Themes and Variations. New York: Macmillan, 1974. 148p. [B]

Needlepoint and bargello are presented in this book, with a full chapter dedicated to technical know-how. A large assortment of beautiful patterns are all shown in color, accompanied on facing pages by clear graphs, making it easy to copy the designs. A very useful workbook.

241 ● Kay, Dorothea. Embroidered Samplers. New York: Scribner, 1980. 127p. [A]

Ten projects are presented in this book, integrated with the history of samplers. The book is suitable for beginners, since the projects are simple and the step-by-step illustrated method of the stitches is easy to understand. Since this volume was first published in England, the list of materials includes mostly English sources. A metric-conversion chart, a bibliography, and a list of suppliers are included.

242 ● Kenyon, Anne. Embroidery and Design on Patterned Fabric. South Brunswick, N.J.: Barnes, 1975. 128p. [D]

The title of this book is misleading, since the author discusses not only embroidery but other types of stitchery, such as quilting, smocking, and appliqué. Various types of patterned fabrics--striped, checked, printed, and woven--are discussed, giving ideas on how to transfer and create patterns with these materials and how to make household articles. Diagrams of the specific stitches accompany the illustrations. Photographs of the finished projects (towel, apron, lampshade, etc.) are included.

243 ● Kerimov, Lyatif. Folk Designs from the Caucasus for Weaving and Needlework. New York: Dover, 1974. 120p. [C]

This is a rich collection of 455 designs on graph paper, easily adaptable to various types of needlework, such as counted cross-stitch, needlepoint, petit-point, latch-hook, or weaving. They have been collected from the Caucasus, which has one of the world's great weaving traditions. Human figures, tortoises, sheep, mythical animals, flowers, and a wealth of other designs from Asiatic and ancient East European sources are presented in the book. They are ready to use for the more experienced needleworker.

244 ● Kerimov, Lyatif. Persian Rug Motifs for Needlepoint; Charted for Easy Use. New York: Dover, 1975. 47p. [D]

This book contains 159 designs from Azerbaijan, a republic of the Soviet Union that borders on Iran. Native rug weavers have been using these motifs for hundreds of years. The designs include stylized birds, human figures, animals, flowers, and numerous geometric forms. Since the designs are printed on charts, they are useful for needlepoint, cross-stitch, embroidery, or rug-hooking. The patterns are in black-and-white, leaving the choice of color combinations to the user.

245 ● Kimmond, Jean, ed. The Anchor Book of European Embroidery. London: Batsford, 1964. 160p. [C]

This book contains some of the most beautiful European designs. The author explains how they can be adapted to British and American practice, and the applications are illustrated with finished projects. The techniques represented include cross-stitch from the Mediterranean, Swedish darning, modern Spanish blackwork, and Hardanger embroidery. The working instructions are well illustrated with

color and black-and-white photographs. The projects include
a wide variety of useful objects, such as cushions (pillows),
runners, and chair covers. This potpourri of techniques
will be useful for those who are already experienced in these
methods.

246 ● Kimmond, Jean. The Coats Book of Modern European
Embroidery. North Pomfret, Vt.: Batsford, 1979.
101p. [B]

Twenty-one examples of "modern" embroidery are
presented here, characterized by bold colors and abstract
designs. However, some of the designs are more traditional than truly modern in style. General technical instructions
and descriptions of the stitches are included, with black-and-
white and some color photographs of the finished projects.

247 ● Kimmond, Jean. Counted Thread Embroidery. New
York: Scribner, 1976. 127p. [C]

Included in this volume are different types of counted-thread embroidery, including cross-stitch, Florentine canvaswork (bargello), gros-point, petit-point, drawn fabric,
Spanish blackwork, and Lagartera. The explanation and diagrams of the various stitches are sufficient, but only experienced needleworkers would be able to follow them. The
thirty-four designs are beautiful, and the author gives the
amount and color of yarns, instructions for working and finishing, a color-keyed graph, and color photograph of the finished project.

248 ● Kimmond, Jean. Embroidery for the Home. London:
Batsford; Newton Centre, Mass.: Branford, 1970.
127p. [C]

The author presents more than thirty patterns for
decoration or other use in the home. They include pillows,
table runners, chair backs, luncheon sets, tablecloths, and
hangings. Among the stitches used are needlepoint, embroidery, pulled work, and Hardanger embroidery. The patterns
are tasteful and original, presented here with charts, close-
up photographs, and color pictures of the finished products.
Instructions are sufficient, but mostly oriented toward the
experienced needleworker.

249 ● King, Bucky. Creative Canvas Embroidery. Rev.
    ed. Great Neck, N.Y.: Hearthside, 1972. 157p.
    [D]

    This complete, easy-to-follow guide for both be-
ginners and advanced needleworkers describes the basic techniques for fifty stitches, which are clearly illustrated with
drawings and color photographs of finished projects. The
book goes beyond the mechanical aspects of other how-to
books, urging readers to use needlework as a creative outlet and design their own pieces. The various applications
are shown in clear photographs of the finished projects, such
as chair seats, pillows, wallets, and purses.

250 ● Klimova, Nina T. Folk Embroidery of the USSR.
    New York: Van Nostrand, 1981. 128p. [C]

    The author presents a collection of embroidery
stitches used in various parts of the Soviet Union. She attempts to combine the history and culture of the land with
the various embroidery techniques, such as cross-stitch,
openwork, and needlepoint. Each technique is explained
very thoroughly and is illustrated with graphs and drawings.
The finished products are shown in color and black-and-white
photographs.

251 ● Kluger, Phyllis. A Needlepoint Gallery of Patterns
    from the Past. New York: Knopf; dist. by Ran-
    dom House, 1975. 191p. [C]

    The author presents 102 designs from over 4,000
years of civilization. Countries and civilizations represented: Ancient Crete, Egypt, Near East, Greece and Rome,
Byzantium, the Middle Ages, Renaissance, seventeenth-nine-
teenth-century Europe, and Colonial America. Each pattern
includes black-and-white photographs of the finished piece,
color-keyed graph, and description of the design's origin.
Suitable mostly for intermediate and advanced needleworkers.

252 ● Kluger, Phyllis. Victorian Designs for Needlepoint.
    New York: Holt, 1978. 86p. [C]

    A handsome collection of Victorian designs, with
charts (color key included) and color photographs of the fin-

ished products. After a short historical introduction, the author presents technical instructions, with a list of different stitches. Each design is shown on graph paper, making it possible to copy the patterns. The designs are attractive, but difficult; only the more experienced should attempt them.

253 ● Kmit, Ann, Johanna Luciou, and Loretta Luciou. Ukrainian Embroidery. New York: Van Nostrand, 1978. 110p. [D]

    This book presents detailed instructions for authentic Ukrainian embroidery. The designs comprise basic, intermediate, and advanced patterns. Besides the necessary technical information, the designs include openwork embroidery, flat stitches, weaving stitches, and cross-stitch. Graphs and photographs (some in color) of many finished products make this book worthwhile for those who like East European and specifically Ukrainian embroidery.

254 ● Krevitsky, Nik. Stitchery, Art and Craft. New York: Van Nostrand, 1966. 132p. [C]

    The author introduces stitchery as a serious art medium for creative expression. Starting with a survey of historical examples, he discusses the relationship between stitches and materials, between stitches and their possible applications to various objects. A modern approach to stitchery, viewing it more as an art form than craft. The illustrations, many in color, are of works by the author or by other artists.

255 ● Krøncke, Grete. Mounting Handicraft; Ideas and Instructions for Assembling and Finishing. New York: Van Nostrand, 1967. 96p. [B]

    The aim of this volume is to show with clear illustrations and step-by-step instructions the very pleasing effects that may be achieved by imaginative mounting of handicraft articles. The scope of the book is extensive, dealing with mounting of collages, various embroidered fabrics, wall hangings, cushions, handbags, book covers, and so on. A useful, practical book for craftspeople and needleworkers.

256 ● Krueger, Glee. A Gallery of American Samplers;
        The Theodore H. Kapnek Collection. New York:
        Dutton, in association with the Museum of Amer-
        ican Folk Art, 1978. 96p. [D]

        A beautiful collection of American samplers dating
from 1678 to 1865. The Kapnek Collection provides the reader with a broad chronological and geographical range of Americana, as worked by schoolgirls over a span of 200 years.
The book is illustrated with 112 examples, the majority of
them in color. There are also many details, enlarged from
the samplers. A rich and unusual collection of samplers.

257 ● Kurten, Nancy Noland. Needlepoint in Miniature.
        New York: Scribner, 1979. 146p. [C]

        This book presents a large variety of projects for
those who collect miniatures. Such items as needlepoint
rugs, chair seats, cushions, and valances are all worked
out in a scale of one inch to the foot. After giving instructions on materials, threads, and needles, the author introduces many projects with complete technical instructions,
graphs, and photographs of the finished pieces. The appendix contains useful ideas on blocking and finishing miniature
needlepoint.

258 ● Landon, Mary Taylor, and Susan Burrows Swan.
        American Crewel Work. New York: Macmillan,
        1970. 192p. [D]

        This volume is both a study of the historical as-
pects of American embroidery, and a guide to the techniques
of crewel. The authors cover various categories besides
crewel, such as canvaswork (needlepoint or bargello), Berlin work, and Turkey work. The second part includes all
the technical aspects--stitches, designing, finishing, and so
on. The last chapter displays designs for contemporary adaptations. The color plates show historical pieces, many from
museums. This is a good book mostly for crewel embroiderers since needlepoint (canvaswork) is discussed only briefly.

259 ● Landsman, Anne Cheek. Needlework Designs from the

American Indians; Traditional Patterns of the Southeastern Tribes.   South Brunswick, N. J. , and New
York: Barnes, 1977.   160p. [A]

The author searched the cultures of the Southeastern tribes of the United States--Cherokee, Creek, Choctaw,
Chickasaw, and Seminole--and has taken more than 100 traditional designs from basketry, pottery, textiles, and other
crafts and adapted them for needlepoint.   Many photographs
illustrate the applications of the designs with easy-to-follow
stitch diagrams, appropriate for beginners.   Included is a
complete set of stitch diagrams for left-handers.   Some 122
authentic designs are presented with all the necessary instructions together with a survey of Southeastern Indian history.

260 ● Lane, Maggie.   Chinese Rugs Designed for Needlepoint.   New York: Scribner, 1975.   99p. [C]

Aiming her book at the advanced needleworker, the
author presents ten authentic Chinese rug patterns.   Included
with each design are finished rug size, type of canvas, origin of design, colors, yarns, graphs, and working directions.
Lane also explains how to make a graph and vary the patterns according to the user's need or taste.   The amount of
yarn (wool) for each rug is listed at the front of the book.

261 ● Lane, Maggie.   Maggie Lane's Needlepoint Pillows.
New York: Scribner, 1976.   86p. [C]

The designs in this book are based on Chinese
motifs, derived from paintings, porcelains, rugs, and textiles.   Many of the designs are reproduced from Lane's
earlier books (Needlepoint by Design and More Needlepoint
by Design).   Selected to make matching pairs, they represent various shapes, such as round, square, oblong, or oc-
tagon.   Thirteen designs are presented with charts on graph
paper and different color combinations.   The first twenty-
five pages contain all the necessary instructions for working
and finishing the needlepoint pillows.   The designs are beautiful but quite elaborate, and therefore are only for needleworkers with experience.

262 ● Lane, Maggie.   More Needlepoint by Design.   New
York: Scribner, 1972.   150p. [C]

In a sequel to her first book, listed below, the author presents twenty new designs, strongly Chinese and Oriental in flavor. After the technical instructions and description of stitches, the beautiful designs are presented with graphs, color keys, and finishing instructions. Most of the designs are quite complex, and are therefore suitable only for more experienced needleworkers.

263 ● Lane, Maggie. Needlepoint by Design: Variations
    on Chinese Themes. New York: Scribner, 1970.
    114p. [A]

This book contains over ninety combinations of designs derived from Chinese art and adapted for needlepoint. The diagrams can be readily transferred to needlepoint canvas. Suggestions are made for practical projects, such as Parsons tables, rugs, pillows, and fashion accessories. Photographs of the finished works (some in color), diagrams, and graphs are very clear. Intended for beginners, the book might also motivate more experienced needleworkers to make their own designs.

264 ● Lane, Maggie. Rugs and Wall Hangings. Photographs
    by R. Lans Christensen. New York: Scribner,
    1976. 161p. [C]

This book is similar in treatment and arrangement to the author's earlier volume (Chinese Rugs Designed for Needlepoint). Lane presents twelve designs--five panels and seven rugs. The projects are presented with easy-to-read graphs, excellent color photographs, amount and colors of yarns, and brief instructions on working details. A separate chapter discusses suggestions for changes that can easily be made in the designs in this book and lists thirty-six stitches that could be substituted in some of the rugs and wall hangings.

265 ● Lang, John. Geometric Designs for Artists and Crafts-
    men. New York: Exposition, 1959. 85p. [B]

A treasure of unusual geometric designs, suitable for various crafts--fabric, wood, metal, leather, and so on. In making geometric designs according to the method originated by Lang, no skill in drawing is necessary because all the designs are made with instruments. Besides the T-square,

a compass, ruling pen, and two triangles are all that is
needed to create designs similar to the 115 contained in
the book. Lang traces the development of geometric designs from the time of the Celts and Moors. A useful and
interesting book for artists, designers, and needleworkers
who try to create original geometric designs.

266 ● Lantz, Sherlee.   Trianglepoint.   New York: Studio-
       Viking, 1976. 141p. [D]

       A useful and innovative book. The author presents
forty-two ancient and modern patterns with color plates, notes,
graphs, and photographs. The instructions are clear and
easy-to-follow. A separate chapter discusses materials and
suppliers. An additional twenty-five "sketchbook" designs
are added, which make the book suitable for both beginners
and the more experienced. A short bibliography is included
at the end.

267 ● Late Victorian Needlework for Victorian Houses; A
       Fascimile of The Lady's Handbook of Fancy Nee-
       dlework.   Watkins Glen, N.Y.:   American Life
       Foundation, 1979.   383p. [C]

       This fascimile reprint of a book originally pub-
lished in London about 1840 includes many techniques, some
unusual and little-used today. The patterns are original Victorian, but the instructions are not always clear. The illustrations are only in black-and-white, and, because of the
small print, difficult to copy. The book has more of a historic than practical value, although experienced needleworkers should be able to copy some of the designs.

268 ● Laury, Jean Ray.   A Treasury of Needlecraft Gifts
       for the New Baby.   New York: Taplinger, 1976.
       191p. [D]

       An extensive collection of modern designs adapted
for many projects useful for the baby (clothing, in the crib,
etc.). All the designs are sufficiently explained and accompanied by charts and black-and-white and some color photographs. The projects include not only needlepoint but many
other techniques, such as quilting, patchwork, embroidery,
and appliqué. Instructions for the techniques are kept to a

minimum, and therefore only experienced needleworkers
would be able to follow them.

269 ● Ley, Sandra. Russian and Other Slavic Embroidery
    Designs. New York: Scribner, 1976. 95p. [C]

    The book contains fifteen attractive projects based
on traditional designs from Russia and other Eastern European countries. The technique is either cross-stitch or embroidery. The articles include table linens, blouses, aprons,
and clothes. Charts or drawings are provided for each design, and color plates show some of the finished products.
More color pictures would have enhanced the book's attractiveness. Instructions are very brief, and so this is a book
only for the more experienced needleworkers.

270 ● Lightbody, Donna M. Introducing Needlepoint. New
    York: Lothrop, 1973. 157p. [A]

    A suitable book for young beginners, with clear,
closeup photographs and numbered diagrams to illustrate the
text, step-by-step. Simple projects, such as pin-cushions,
eyeglass cases, and coasters, serve as samples on which
to practice each stitch. A glossary, a metric-conversion
chart, and a list of suppliers are appended.

271 ● Lindberg Press. Scandinavian Charted Designs from
    the Archives of the Lindberg Press. New York:
    Dover, 1979. 48p. [B]

    Designs from Scandinavia are famous for their sub-
tle blending of elegance and simplicity. Fifty-six examples
are presented in this book, with easy-to-follow charts, color
codes, and short, basic instructions. The designs can be
used for cross-stitch, needlepoint, or latch-hook. Since instructions are kept to a minimum, some experience will be
needed in using this book.

272 ● Loeb, Marcia. Pennsylvania Dutch Needlepoint De-
    signs, Charted for Easy Use. New York: Dover,
    1976. 48p. [B]

    Fifty authentic designs are presented here. The

patterns, suitable for such items as pillows, belts, or hangings, include the characteristic Pennsylvania Dutch motifs--
tulips, hearts, birds, parrots, hex symbols, and so on.   The
book also contains a full alphabet and a list of numerals.
Taken from old chests, quilts, plates, and other artifacts,
each motif has been adapted by Loeb and charted for use on
#10 needlepoint canvas.   Twenty-two designs are rendered
in full color on the covers.

273 ● The McCall's Book of Rugmaking.   By the editors of
        McCall's Needlework and Crafts magazine.   New
        York: Simon and Schuster, 1976.   168p. [C]

        The editors present nine rugmaking techniques, ar-
ranged in chapters by technique, including needlepoint, latch-
hook, punch needle, weaving, knitting, and appliquéd rugs.
For each technique, instructions and graphs for copying the
design are included.   The finished products are shown in
color plates.   A comprehensive book on rugmaking, with all
necessary details.   The projects are very attractive, but
their execution calls for some experience.

274 ● McCall's Embroidery with Step-by-Step Lessons for
        Beginners; 65 Stitches to Learn and Use.   By the
        editors of McCall's Needlework and Crafts maga-
        zine.   New York: McCall Pattern Co., 1971.
        80p. [A]

        In this basic book for beginners, with clear, easy-
to-follow instructions, the projects are simple and illustrated
in color, and the details are shown on charts or graphs.
The projects are worked in various embroidery stitches, including cross-stitch.   The designs range from traditional to
modern.   The projects include such items as pillows, chair
seats, rugs, hangings, and tote-bags.   Instructions on finishing, joining, stretching, and other practical matters are
included.

275 ● McCall's Needlepoint with Step-by-Step Lessons for
        Beginners; 31 Stitches to Learn and Use.   By the
        editors of McCall's Needlework and Crafts maga-
        zine.   New York: McCall Pattern Co., 1971.   80p.
        [A]

        A basic guide for needlepoint, very similar in format and arrangement to the previous entry, dealing with embroidery. The stitches are fully explained and illustrated with clear charts. The projects are simple, with descriptions, charts, and color photographs of the finished designs. The projects include the usual items for needlepoint--pillows, chair covers, rugs, hangings, and so on. A basic, easy-to-use guide for beginners.

276 ● McClennen, Barbara C. Crewel Embroidery Made Easy. Garden City, N.Y.: Doubleday, 1972. 179p. [D]

This book should appeal to young adults, but also to anyone who attempts to use embroidery as a creative outlet. The author relates the history of crewel, describes its modern uses, and presents practical instructions for selecting materials, drawing your own design, and how to improvise many of the listed sketches. Detailed instructions include three different techniques: wool sculpturing (actually a derivative of stumpwork), breakaway stitchery (the author's own invention), and collage crewel. Although these techniques are unusual, the designs can be used for "simple" embroidery by beginners or more experienced needleworkers. A glossary of stitches is appended.

277 ● McNeill, Moyra. Pulled Thread Embroidery. New York: Taplinger, 1971. 207p. [B]

This book is a basic guide for learning a technique that is undergoing a revival. The author demonstrates how these traditional stitches can be modified to create original designs for personal or household items. The stitches are diagrammed on squared grids, enabling the user to understand how the stitches are worked. Some experience in needlework is necessary for this type of technique.

278 ● Marein, Shirley. Creating Rugs and Wall Hangings; A Complete Guide. Renderings by Eleanor Bello; photographs by Alan Sweetman. London: Studio Vista, 1975. 222p. [D]

Complete, detailed description of various techniques used to make rugs. The techniques include weaving, knotting, hooking, embroidering, crochet, and knitting. Since the book is an English publication, the term "embroidery"

is used to refer to needlepoint. A whole chapter is devoted
to this technique. A wealth of technical information, practical hints, and photographs makes this volume a useful workbook and a guide to rugmaking techniques.

279 ● Marein, Shirley. Flowers in Design; A Guide for
      Stitchery and Fabric Crafts. New York: Viking,
      1973. 172p. [C]

The main subjects of this book are floral forms,
and the author explains and illustrates how these have been
interpreted in a multitude of ways throughout history. Here
are representations of Renaissance paintings, Islamic build-
ings, Venetian laces, Turkish carpets, Chinese embroideries,
Victorian needlework, American quilts, and many more ways
in which flower motifs have been used. The wealth of illustrations make the book a rich source of ideas for creating
new designs on floral themes for a variety of fabrics. There
are instructions for translating these elements into workable
designs.

280 ● Marein, Shirley. Oriental Images; New Designs for
      Needlepoint and Stitchery. New York: Viking,
      1978. 159p. [B]

A collection of original designs inspired by Oriental
art, with patterns graphed for needlepoint or ready to copy
for embroidery, rug-hooking, appliqué, and patchwork. Examples of the finished work are shown in color, and color
charts accompany the designs wherever they are appropriate.
Photographs show the works of art that inspired the design.
Methods of copying and enlarging designs and transferring
them to cloth or canvas are also demonstrated.

281 ● Marein, Shirley. Stitchery; Needlepoint, Appliqué,
      and Patchwork; A Complete Guide. Renderings
      by Eleanor Bello; photographs by Alan Sweetman.
      New York: Viking, 1974. 207p. [D]

This book covers several types of techniques. The
author fully explains in detail how to master these techniques,
how to do your own designing, and how to adapt designs to
the use of various materials. More than 200 drawings, diagrams, and photographs (some in color) illustrate the text.
A good, basic guide.

282 ● Markrich, Lilo. Principles of the Stitch. Chicago:
Regnery, 1976. 122p. [D]

The emphasis in this book is strictly on stitches.
The author reduces needlework stitches to a few simple
groups and explains how to use them most effectively. Flat
stitches, wrapped stitches, cross-stitches, and composite
stitches are fully discussed and also placed in historical context to promote a complete understanding of their potential.
Comprehensive sections on use of color, texture, and patterns complement the practical advice on where to find designs and how to turn them into individual pieces. Stitch
diagrams, as well as full-color and black-and-white pictures,
are included.

283 ● Markrich, Lilo, and Heinz Edgar Kiewe. Victorian
Fancywork; 19th Century Needlepoint Patterns and
Designs. Chicago: Regnery, 1974. 172p. [C]

After discussing the social background and the role
of women in Victorian times, the authors present original
Victorian designs, suitable for needlepoint, cross-stitch, or
filet work. Some of the designs are enlarged for easy copying. Technical instructions are clear and sufficiently full.
The illustrations are mostly in black-and-white, with a few
color plates. The designs are beautiful, but because they
are elaborate, they are only for experienced needleworkers.

284 ● Martin, Mary. Mary Martin's Needlepoint. New
York: Morrow, 1969. 148p. [C]

This is the story of how Mary Martin became interested in needlepoint and how she used it as a relaxation
between her demanding stage appearances. Starting with a
rug for her living room and continuing with pillows, wall
panels, purses, and chair covers, she describes how each
project originated and became connected either with her thea-
trical work or with her home. Thirty-seven color plates
and many black-and-white photographs illustrate her versatility in needlepoint. She prefers original designs, adapted
to the decor, style, and color in her home. In the final
chapter, she discusses designs, canvas types, stitches, and
colors, giving advice and encouragement both to the novice
and to the more experienced needleworker.

285 ● Marton, Sheila Nassberg, and Muriel Brandwein Sel-
    ick. Patterned Backgrounds for Needlepoint. New
    York: Van Nostrand, 1977. 100p. [D]

This book deals with a specific part of needlepoint,
the background. To break up the monotony of a large, solid
area, the authors offer a great variety of backgrounds to
complement the central motif. Over 200 designs are presented in this book. They are divided into four levels of
complexity, and samples of each are shown. A full-color
portfolio demonstrates the completed projects. A source of
inspiration for needleworkers, textile designers, and craftspeople.

286 ● Mason, Enid. Embroidery Designs for Students of
    All Ages. Newton Centre, Mass.: Branford,
    1968. 128p. [A]

Written for the student and the young teacher, this
book presents designs that are adaptable for many types of
needlework. It is not a workbook because projects are not
included, only forms and patterns (mostly in modernistic
vein). The many forms can be adapted by the reader to
various materials, techniques, or purposes. A book of ideas
for the artistic self-expression of students.

287 ● Mathews, Sibyl I. Charted Designs for Needle-made
    Rugs. New York: Hearthside, 1968. 150p. [C]

This volume presents forty-six charted designs for
rugs, including motifs from various countries, such as England, France, Greece, Turkey, Iran, and China. Technical
instructions have been kept to a minimum, but each chart
is accompanied by notes recommending stitches and colors.
A rich collection of rug patterns adapted to needlework, basically in the "tent" stitch. Since patterns are very complicated, this book is only for more advanced needleworkers.

288 ● Mathews, Sibyl I. Needle-made Rugs. Rev. ed.
    London: Mills and Boon, 1967. 128p. [D]

In this book, Mathews tries to cover everything
that one has to know about making needleworked rugs. After
a short history, materials and methods are discussed. The

second half of the book presents specific designs, illustrated on graph paper (some folded, because of size). Specific rugs are discussed separately, including church rugs
and carpets. A few Oriental rugs are shown on color plates.
A good source for all information about rugmaking with the
needle, using a variety of needlepoint stitches. The level
of difficulty ranges from the simple to the elaborate.

289 ● May, Marian. Decorative Stitchery. Menlo Park,
     Calif.: Lane, 1970 © 1965). 80p. [D]

     After an introductory chapter of basic instructions
and a stitch chart, the author discusses various embroidery
techniques, such as crewel, Swedish and Mexican embroidery,
and blackwork. Each type is represented by a project, giving the description and working methods. The second part
of the book, arranged like the first, is devoted to appliqué,
both by hand and by machine. The many useful and decorative projects range from easy to complicated.

290 ● Meilach, Dona Z., and Lee Erlin Snow. Creative
     Stitchery. New York: Galahad, 1969. 118p. [C]

     Stitchery is presented here as an art form, much
more than just the simple embroidery accepted as a basic
home craft. The book is an illustrated presentation of the
techniques and methods employed in this medium. After
the usual technical information, the authors cover such top-
ics as multiple fabrics, working on a frame, mixed media
and stitchery, and sculptured stitchery. The book concludes
with a list of sources for materials. A valuable work for
art teachers and artists, as well as those who wish to use
stitchery as a hobby or for creative expression.

291 ● Meilach, Dona Z., and Dee Menagh. Exotic Needle-
     work with Ethnic Patterns, Techniques, Inspira-
     tions. New York: Crown, 1978. 280p. [C]

     This book shows how to adapt patterns and unusual
motifs of other cultures for today's needlework. There are
basic instructions for embroidery, giving detailed descriptions of various stitches. Other chapters discuss other techniques, such as appliqué, patchwork, beadwork, working with
silver and gold thread, smocking, and crochet. The last
chapter presents patterns for garments with ethnic designs
in embroidery and other techniques. The book contains 410

photographs, 208 drawings, and twenty color plates. Among
the patterns are Indian, Oriental, African, Mexican, and
South American designs, all adaptable for modern use. An
unusual workbook, with a wealth of ideas for the experienced
embroiderer.

292 ● Merrill, Virginia, and Jean Jessop. Needlework in
    Miniature: Techniques and Inspirations for Making
    Miniature Rugs, Upholstery, Pillows, Bedspreads,
    Bed Trimmings, Doll Clothes and Many More. New
    York: Crown, 1978. 198p. [C]

        The authors feature unusual charted designs, based
on historical patterns for rugs and other dollhouse accessories. An interesting feature of the book is the many designs
for miniature military figures. Petit-point is completely
covered, but the treatment of the other techniques is far
less complete.

293 ● Messent, Jan. Designing for Needlepoint and Em-
    broidery from Ancient and Primitive Sources. New
    York: Macmillan, 1976. 127p. [B]

        The art of ancient civilizations, ethnic sources,
and signs, symbols, and objects are briefly surveyed in this
book. The description of the various stitches is clear and
easy-to-follow. The usual technical aspects are also discussed in detail. The author gives instructions on how to
adapt primitive designs to a variety of fabrics and modern
uses.

294 ● Messent, Jan. Embroidery and Nature. Watertown,
    Mass.: Branford, 1980. 168p. [C]

        This work is more useful as a source of inspira-
tion than as a how-to instruction book. The author offers
a rich selection of designs from animal, mineral, and plant
models, presented in different techniques. There are few
sketches and graphs, but a wealth of photographs of finished
projects that can be used for embroidery ideas.

295 ● Meulenbelt-Nieuwburg, Albarta, comp. Embroidery

Motifs from Old Dutch Samplers. New York: Scribner, 1975. 192p. [D]

Each chapter in this book is devoted to a particular motif--flowers, birds, animals, hearts, houses, and household goods. Reproductions of samplers from museum and private collections, which form a substantial part of the book, are accompanied by easy-to-follow graphs and drawings. In the final chapter, the author gives directions for making a sampler.

296 ● Meyer, Carolyn. Stitch by Stitch: Needlework for Beginners. New York: Harcourt, 1970. 93p. [A]

This guide for beginners, with clear diagrams and easy-to-follow instructions, is devoted primarily to basic embroidery stitches but also covers appliqué and needlepoint. Following each section on a different stitch are projects utilizing this stitch on such useful objects as placemats, pot holders, pillows, and pincushions. This volume is intended primarily for children, but adults can also utilize its basic instructions and projects.

297 ● Miller, Irene Preston, and Winifred Lubell. The Stitchery Book; Embroidery for Beginners. Garden City, N.Y.: Doubleday, 1965. 96p. [D]

The title is somewhat misleading, since the book contains projects not only for beginners but also for more experienced needleworkers. The authors use mostly free-form stitches for modern applications. A few designs are in cross-stitch or crewel. Technical instructions are elaborate, with black-and-blue illustrations and many photographs, some in color. The book contains a large number of projects; many are suitable for young people, others for the more experienced.

298 ● Morris, Barbara. Victorian Embroidery. New York: Nelson, 1962. 238p. [C]

This is not the usual how-to book but rather a historical essay on English embroidery, covering Victorian domestic and church embroidery from the 1830s until 1901. The author based her work on a firsthand study of surviving examples, supplemented by extensive reference to contemporary periodicals and pattern books.   For collectors, this volume, illustrated with many photographs, will be of special value in identifying and dating existing specimens. For needleworkers, it can be used as a source of ideas and unusual projects.

299 ● Mortellito, Nina.   Needlepoint for the Whole Family. New York: Walker, 1973.   192p. [D]

   A brief history of needlework introduces the reader to the needle arts of the past as well as to present trends. The basic stitches are very clearly explained, presented not only with diagrams but with numbers, allowing readers to follow with the needle.   The designs are varied and can be used for many occasions and purposes.   The author also describes the subtle effects of shading technique, or "painting with needle and thread."   Suggestions for variations are included with each design.   The last chapter, "An Illustrated Dictionary," gives the reader a handy reference section of basic terminology.   A short bibliography and a list of suppliers are appended.

300 ● Musheno, Elizabeth J.   Book of Colonial Needlework: A Handbook of Contemporary Projects; Crewelwork, Whitework, Edgestitching, Fagoting, Drawnwork, Stumpwork, Turkeywork, Candlewicking, Appliqué, Patchwork, Hooking, Crochet, Braiding.   New York: Van Nostrand, 1975.   136p. [C]

   Thirteen types of needlecraft are described in detail, with instructions on fabrics, threads, yarns, design, and equipment.   The author describes some forms of stitchery that are rarely used today. The explanations in some cases are not easy to follow, making this book suitable only for more advanced needleworkers.

301 ● Myers, Carole Robbins.   A Primer of Left-handed Embroidery.   New York: Scribner, 1974.   158p. [D]

   This book is devoted entirely to the needs of left-handed people.   Directions are given for fifty-five stitches and illustrated with an ingenious type of diagram that uses a system of dots, numbered consecutively.   The stitches, arranged in seven main groups, offer a wide choice for the left-handed embroiderer.

302 ● The Needleworker's Constant Companion; Step-by-Step Instructions with Hundreds of Projects, for Dress-making, Sewing for the Home, Knitting Plain and Fancy, and All Kinds of Crocheting. Edited by Susannah Read. New York: Viking, 1978. 352p. [D]

Although not mentioned in the title, this compre-hensive treatment of all kinds of needlework devotes about seventy pages to needlepoint, bargello, blackwork, and other types of embroidery. The rest of the book is devoted to sew-ing, knitting, and crochet. It contains a wealth of informa-tion, giving instructions in every aspect of the basic tech-niques, including possible difficulties. The patterns are pre-sented with many color and black-and-white illustrations. A useful book for both beginners and advanced needleworkers.

303 ● Ness, Pamela Miller. Assisi Embroidery; Techniques and 42 Charted Designs. New York: Dover, 1979. 48p. [B]

This book discusses Assisi embroidery, which is basically a form of counted-thread work (needlepoint) in which the design is outlined in silhouette and the background is filled in. The author presents a short history of this type of work, the techniques, and forty-two charted designs. The color photographs of the projects are shown on the front and back covers.

304 ● Ness, Pamela Miller. Swedish Tvistsom Embroidery. New York: Dover, 1981. 48p. [B]

Tvistsom is an attractive form of folk embroidery that has been practiced in Sweden since the seventeenth cen-tury. It is worked in long-arm cross-stitch, creating a dur-able and functional texture. This book contains forty-six charted designs, with basic instructions for various projects, such as clothing, tablecloths, pillows, and hangings. A very useful book for an unusual technique.

305 ● Newman, Thelma R. The Complete Cross-Stitch; 52

Stitches in Embroidery and Gross Point in New and Traditional Designs and Methods. New York: Crown, 1978. 214p. [D]

The author devotes this book to the ubiquitous cross-stitch, discussing its origin, development, and materials. She presents fifty-two stitches with diagrams, from the simple to the most complicated. A large collection of patterns is included with graphs and instructions for easy applications or further creative use. The last chapter offers directions for blocking, finishing, and mounting the project. A complete guide to the cross-stitch technique.

306 ● Newnes Complete Needlecraft. London: Hamlyn, 1972 © 1969). 248p. [C]

The book covers many types of needlecraft, such as embroidery, patchwork, rugmaking, knitting, crochet, dressmaking, and gift-making. There are over 200 diagrams and photographs and sixteen pages of color plates to illustrate the projects. Since the book attempts to cover many types of needlework, basic instructions are kept to the minimum. Only experienced needleworkers should try these projects.

307 ● Nicholson, Joan. Canvas Work Simplified. New York: Arco, 1973. 96p. [D]

The author presents in this book twenty-four projects in full color, with sketches, diagrams, and technical instructions (finishing, framing, etc.). Half-cross-stitch (or tent stitch) is the only one used for all designs. Besides the projects--which include such items as belts, purses, boxes, pillows, and picture frames--Nicholson offers a collection of designs (geometric, fur patterns, floral) to inspire needleworkers to create their own pieces.

308 ● Nicholson, Joan. Creative Embroidery. New York: Gramercy, 1960. 128p. [D]

Traditional methods are combined in this volume with new materials to produce embroidery suitable for today's living. Both the basic and the more complicated stitches are clearly described and illustrated with drawings and photographs. The emphasis is on creativity, and the author explains how these designs can be adapted for various projects.

309 ● Nicoletti, Sally. Japanese Motifs for Needlepoint. New York: Morrow, 1981. 128p. [C]

The author created thirty patterns, using the motifs of Japanese clothing, especially No theater costumes. Each of the patterns is described in detail, with history of the motif, graphs, and a black-and-white photo of the finished project. Instructions on canvas, stitches, and yarns are clear and easy to follow. Since only the basics of the techniques are explained, the book is not suitable for beginners.

310 ● Nicoletti, Sally. Weaving Designs for Needlepoint. New York: Morrow, 1978. 182p. [D]

The book presents a great wealth of weaving patterns adapted for needlepoint designs. The author selected the patterns from many sources, including museum textiles and from many nations and periods. The sixty-three projects are each accompanied by an easy-to-copy graph. There are thirty-two color plates and eighty black-and-white photographs of the finished projects, which include mostly pillows, handbags, and chair covers. This is a workbook, but it can also be used as inspiration for original designs.

311 ● Nielsen, Edith. Scandinavian Embroidery, Past and Present. New York: Scribner, 1978. 174p. [D]

This comprehensive book relates the history of Scandinavian embroidery from 1700 to the present, showing the various traditions that developed in each country. Two unique styles, Hardanger and Hedebo, are fully explained. Other techniques include cross-stitch, needlepoint, crewel, and straight embroidery. The designs are fully explained and illustrated with diagrams. The historical essay is accompanied by photographs of many original pieces. A good, basic book on all types of Scandinavian embroidery.

312 ● Norbury, James. Counted-Thread Embroidery on

Linens and Canvas. New York: Studio, 1956.
96p. [B]

This book by a British author presents several
kinds of counted-thread embroidery, including cross-stitch,
needlepoint, and bargello. Norbury explains each type in
detail, giving a great variety of stitches with practical applications. The finished projects are presented in black-
and-white or color photographs. A good working book, with
a great variety of patterns and stitches.

313 ● Oleson, Karen E. Floral Patterns for Needlecraft
and the Decorative Arts. New York: Van Nostrand. 1978. 208p. [C]

The author provides ninety-three designs, each in
two sizes for easy tracing and transfer. These designs are
based on her research on tapestries and other museum pieces
and, among others, Walcott watercolors in the National Collection of Fine Arts. Besides the usual technical instructions, the book's individuality lies in its unique patterns.
A rich selection of floral patterns is presented, providing
a source of inspiration for those who like flowers in needlecraft.

314 ● Olsen, Mary P. For the Greater Glory; A Church
Needlepoint Handbook. New York: Seabury/Cross-
road, 1980. 200p. [C]

The author humorously describes her experience
as leader of a 400-piece needlepoint project for the St. James
Episcopal Church in Keene, N.H. She discusses every detail of the project, helping the readers to use their own imagination in developing different designs. A list of sources
(with addresses), a glossary, and a bibliography are appended.

315-334 ● Ondori Publishing Co., Tokyo.

These Japanese publications appeared on the American market during the seventies. Several of them deal with
embroidery. Since their format and arrangement are similar, they are listed below in alphabetical order. In all
Ondori books, the emphasis is on patterns, and technical

instructions are kept to a minimum.   The designs are accompanied by clear, easy-to-follow charts and drawings.
The finished products are illustrated on color plates.   The
designs are European in style, ranging from the sophisticated to the primitive.   The technique is almost exclusively
embroidery, with several books devoted to one particular
type--cross-stitch.   Because these publications are basically
pattern books, only needleworkers with experience can use
them. [C]

315 ● Beautiful Embroidery Designs.   Tokyo: Ondorisha;
        New York: Kodansha; dist. by Harper, 1981.
        103p.

316 ● A Collection of Designs for Cross-Stitch.   Tokyo: On-
        dorisha; New York: Kodansha; dist. by Harper,
        1980.   96p.

317 ● Creative Embroidery Designs.   Tokyo: Ondorisha,
        1978.   104p.

318 ● Cross-Stitch Designs.   Tokyo: Ondorisha, 1975.   98p.

319 ● Cross-Stitch Patterns.   By the Ondori Publications Co.
        staff and Misiko Murayama.   Tokyo: Ondori, 1976.
        64p.

320 ● Cross-Stitch Small Designs.   Tokyo: Ondorisha, 1977.
        108p.

321 ● Easy Embroidery.   Tokyo: Ondori, 1974.   81p.

322 ● Embroidery Designs.   Tokyo: Ondori, 1974.   64p.

323 ● Embroidery for Beginners.   Tokyo: Ondorisha; dist.
        by Japan Publ. Trading Co. (Elmsford, N.Y.),
        1977.   104p.

324 ● Embroidery for Children's Clothing.   Tokyo: Ondor-
        isha; dist. by Japan Publ. Trading Co. (Elmsford,
        N.Y.), 1977.   102p.

325 ● Embroidery for Fun.   Tokyo: Ondorisha, 1974.   136p.

326 ● The Embroidery of Roses.   Tokyo: Ondori, New
        York: Kodansha, dist. by Harper, 1980.   143p.

327 ● Floral Embroidery.   Tokyo: Ondori, 1975.   72p.

328 ● Lovely Embroidery Patterns. Tokyo: Ondorisha,
New York: Kodansha; dist. by Harper, 1979.
96p.

329 ● One-Point Embroidery and Appliqué. New ed. Tokyo:
Ondori, 1977. 88p.

330 ● Simple Cross-Stitch. Tokyo: Ondorisha, 1976. 103p.

331 ● Simple Embroidery. Tokyo: Ondori, 1976. 72p.

332 ● Small Flowers in Embroidery. Tokyo: Ondorisha,
1976. 104p.

333 ● Stitches and Samplers. Tokyo: Ondori, 1974. 105p.

334 ● A Treasury of Embroidery Samplers. Tokyo: Ondorisha; New York: Kodansha; dist. by Harper,
1981. 97p.

335 ● Ormond, Brande. American Primitives in Needlepoint. Boston: Houghton Mifflin, 1977. 139p. [B]

Eleven masterpieces of American primitive paintings are here adapted to needlepoint. The author tried to
transcribe the originals faithfully and graph them clearly.
Any moderately adept needleworker can transform them onto
canvas. After the technical instructions, the finished projects are shown in color photographs. A collection of patterns for borders and alphabets make this book a useful volume for those who like American folk art.

336 ● Ormond, Brande. Museum Masterpieces in Needlepoint. Text by Marion Muller. Boston: Houghton
Mifflin, 1978. 127p. [D]

Works of famous artists are transferred into needlepoint in this book. The selection covers various periods
in art history and range in difficulty from the easy to the
advanced. Each canvas is presented with graphs and accompanied by a short essay on the artist, the period, and
the specific piece. In addition to several Matisses, the
twelve pieces include paintings by Van Gogh, Braque, and
Gauguin; an Egyptian wall painting; a Greek vase; and an
Islamic miniature. Unfortunately, only a few projects are
illustrated in color.

337 ● Ormond, Brande. Needlepoints to Go; Small Projects
        for Spare Moments. Boston: Houghton Mifflin,
        1975. 107p. [B]

    A collection of original designs, including belts,
coasters, small picture frames, purses, and totebags. Each
design is drawn to its exact size on canvas-scale graph paper and also shown in full color. The projects can be worked
by tracing the outline or by counting stitches, according to
the reader's preference. Complete finishing instructions
follow each item. The patterns represent a variety of styles
--Oriental, modern, Art Nouveau, and traditional. A very
practical workbook for small projects.

338 ● Orr, Anne. Anne Orr's Charted Designs. New York:
        Dover, 1978. 40p. [C]

    This collection of 203 designs, published in cooper-
ation with the Center for the History of American Needlework,
presents Orr's best designs, charted exactly as they appeared
in her original books. There is a special color section (eight
pages) with eighty-seven designs, and the finished products appear in color on the inside covers. The designs may be
used for any needlework techniques, worked over counted
threads or in blocks--e.g., in cross-stitch, needlepoint,
filet and mosaic crochet, petit-point, latch-hook, or quilting,
made from tiny squares. Advanced artisans can use these
patterns for many techniques. A rich collection of beautiful
designs for the more experienced needleworker.

339 ● Orr, Jan. Now Needlepoint; A Joyous New Approach
        to Creative Designing. New York: Van Nostrand,
        1975. 208p. [A]

    Every project in this book is based on five types
of simple stitches that the author calls the "now" needlepoint. Using only large-mesh canvas, she describes each
project from start to finish with step-by-step instructions.
Black-and-white photographs and drawings illustrate each
project.

340 ● Pakula, Marion Broome. Needlepoint Plaids. New
        York: Crown, 1975. 96p. [C]

    Pakula worked out an ingenious, but simple, for-

mula for creating plaids by numbered patterns. With this
method, it is possible to take any combination of numbers
and work a plaid from it. Chapters give examples of simple plaid patterns with suggested color combinations. Authentic Scotch tartan patterns are adapted to needlepoint, and
others have been designed by the author. Each patterns is
presented in color, with photographs and suggestions for
practical applications. An unusual use of needlepoint. No
basic instructions are included here, so therefore this book
is not for beginners.

341 ● Pakula, Marion Broome, and Rhoda Ochser Goldberg.
Needlepoint Patterns for Signs and Sayings. New
York: Crown, 1977. 80p. [B]

Many patterns and signs are included in this book,
which will appeal to many types of people. The designs are
suitable for almost every room in the house, the office, or
any other place you like. Adapted to needlepoint or cross-
stitch, they are mostly simple, easy-to-follow designs, illustrated with graphs and black-and-white pictures. Some
designs are shown in color on the cover of the book.

342 ● Paludan, Lis. Easy Embroidery. Translated by
Christine Crowley. New York: Taplinger, 1975.
125p. [A]

Intended for all ages, but suitable mostly for children, this volume provides information on materials, supplies,
starting and completing the embroidery, pattern transfers,
methods, and stitches. Although the organization of the book
is little confused, the material is well presented, not only
on embroidery but on appliqué and fabric printing. Twenty
embroidery stitches are illustrated with black-and-white and
color photographs. Thirty-two pages of patterns are included
at the end of the book.

343 ● Parker, Betty, and Edith Martin. Embroidery Magic
on Patterned Fabrics. New York: Scribner, 1976.
116p. [C]

As the title implies, the topic is embroidery on
patterned fabrics, a subject not fully covered in other needlework books. A wealth of materials and projects is dis-

played, with technical instructions, drawings, and photographs (some in color). Since the patterns are not easy, the book is suitable mostly for the experienced. A glossary of stitches is included.

344 ● Parker, Elinor Milner. Letters and Numbers for Needlepoint. New York: Scribner, 1978. 93p. [A]

Numbers and letters of the alphabet are presented in various sizes and formats designed for needlepoint and cross-stitch. The text has been kept to a minimum in this book, the body of which consists of easy-to-copy charts. Good workbook for beginners who want to use letters or numbers in their projects.

345 ● Parker, Xenia Ley. A Beginner's Book of Needlepoint and Embroidery. New York: Dodd, Mead, 1975. 160p. [A]

This useful guide for the beginner provides information on every possible aspect of needlework, even subjects that are either absent or superficially treated in many books. The author treats needlepoint and bargello separately from crewel and embroidery. She illustrates the text with clear graphics of nineteen needlepoint stitches, six bargello patterns, and twenty-two embroidery stitches. The final chapter contains introductory projects, both challenging and practical.

346 ● Perrone, Lisbeth. Lisbeth Perrone's Folk Art in Needlepoint and Cross-Stitch. New York: Random House, 1978. 96p. [D]

Based on a year's work at the Museum of International Folk Art in Santa Fe, the author presents a wealth of designs from Europe, Asia, the Americas, and Africa. Each design is marked according to level of difficulty. Directions and charts are clear and easy to follow. Practical advice is given on selection of colors and possible applications for modern use.

347 ● Perrone, Lisabeth. Lisbeth Perrone's Needlepoint

Workbook.   New York: Random House, 1973.
48p. [A]

This book, printed in unusually large format, offers forty-eight designs for pillows or pictures.   The designs are in their original size, ready to be copied by the
user.   The introduction is short but very clear and to the
point.   Each finished project is shown in a color photograph.
The designs are mostly in traditional style, with a few modernistic ones.   This ready-made workbook would save the
expense of a commercial kit, even for the beginner.

348 ● Perrone, Lisbeth.   The New World of Crewel.   New
York: Random House, 1975.   112p. [D]

With an organization very similar to her earlier
book, The New World of Needlepoint, Perrone explains the
fundamentals of crewel embroidery and provides about fifty
designs, mostly traditional, but a few original.   Very clear,
precise diagrams and instructions for the various stitches,
indicating for each project the level of difficulty.

349 ● Perrone, Lisbeth.   The New World of Needlepoint;
101 Exciting Designs in Bargello, Quickpoint, Gros-
point, and Other Repeat Patterns.   New York: Random House, 1972.   142p. [D]

After a short introduction about the technical aspects of needlework and descriptions of the basic stitches,
Perrone presents 101 beautiful designs.   Attached to each
design is a two-color (black-and-blue) chart and a black-
and-white photograph of the actual pattern.   The finished
products are shown in full-color photographs.   The projects
are marked according to their difficulty, from easy to advanced.   The patterns are mostly suitable for pillows, but
they can be easily adapted for other items.   An excellent
workbook with beautiful, easy-to-copy patterns for every
type of needlepoint project.

350 ● Perrone, Lisbeth.   Walt Disney Characters Needlepoint Book: Embroideries and Needlework Instructions.   New York: Random House, 1976.   95p. [A]

Mickey and Minnie Mouse, Donald Duck, Pinocchio,

and other Disney characters are presented here for application in needlework projects, such as pillows, stools, trays,
and baskets.   Perrone provides all the necessary practical
instructions from start to finish.   The Disney studio contributed the full-size designs.   All the patterns are easy to
work and suitable for beginners.

351 ● Petersen, Grete.   Borders for Embroidery.   Trans-
         lated by Anne Wilkins.   New York: Van Nostrand,
         1973.   63p. [D]

     Borders, traditional and modern, from many lands
make up the material of this book.   Illustrated in two colors
(black and blue), some 230 examples can be worked with different methods and materials (cross-stitch, embroidery, wool,
silk, beads, etc.) The book could also be extremely useful
as a source of motifs for other crafts that use borders, such
as weaving, fabric-printing, lacemaking, and so on.

352 ● Petersen, Grete, and Elsie Svennas.   Handbook of
         Stitches: 200 Embroidery Stitches, Old and New,
         with Descriptions, Diagrams and Samplers.   New
         York: Van Nostrand, 1970.   64p. [C]

     This extremely compact embroidery handbook,
translated from the Danish, presents over 200 embroidery stitches and styles.   The diagrams and accompanying photographs
are clear, but the text is minimal.   A rich source of material for the experienced, but beginners can use the patterns
with the help of a basic guide that provides more technical
information.

353 ● Petrakis, Joan.   The Needle Arts of Greece; Design
         and Techniques.   New York: Scribner, 1977.   175p.
         [C]

     This book brings together a variety of designs from
all parts of Greece--the mainland, the Aegean and Ionian is-
lands, and Crete.   The needleworker can find here a great
wealth of unique and fascinating designs, from geometric and
abstract patterns to birds, flowers, and borders.   All can
be adapted to needlepoint, crewel, blackwork, and whitework.
Full directions are included for each project, with diagrams
and photographs, some in color.

354 ● Picken, Mary Brooks, and Doris White. Needlepoint
   Made Easy. New York: Harper, 1955. 149p. [A]

   A basic guide about every aspect of needlepoint--
stitches, blocking, finishing, and so on. Additional chapters
discuss children and needlepoint, needlepoint as occupational
therapy, family records in needlepoint, and making your own
design. Illustrations are only in black-and-white. Not a
workbook, but a basic guide, very helpful for every beginner.

355 ● Projansky, Ella. Sculptured Needlepoint Stitchery.
   New York: Scribner, 1978. 132p. [C]

   Contains designs with a three-dimensional sculptured look and many interesting combinations of smooth and
textured stitches. There are complete directions for twenty-
four projects, including easy-to-read charts and keys to color
combinations. The projects comprise a variety of pillows
and pincushions, a footstool, and a mirror frame. The text
is supplemented by full-color and black-and-white photographs.

356 ● Ramazangolu, Gülseren. Turkish Embroidery. New
   York: Van Nostrand, 1976. 104p. [C]

   The use of gold, silver, and silk threads and pad-
ded (raised) stitches characterize Turkish embroidery, presented in this book. The author describes thirty-five stitches
from the embroidery traditions of her country, adhering faithfully to the colors and floral designs of Turkish style. Technical instructions and illustrations are sufficient, but only an
experienced needleworker should attempt this type of work.
A bibliography and a list of suppliers are appended.

357 ● Raynor, Louise A., and Carolyn H. Kerr. Church
   Needlepoint; Patterns and Instructions. Wilton,
   Conn.: Morehouse-Barlow, 1976. 75p. [C]

   Thirty-eight designs appropriate for churches are
presented in this book, each drawn on graph paper for easy
copying. The finished designs are illustrated in color. Brief
technical instructions, including stitches, layout, finishing,
and so forth, are included. The authors leave the actual
planning of the project to the ingenuity of the user. A handy
volume for church embroidery.

358 ● Rhodes, Mary. Ideas for Canvas Work. Newton Centre, Mass.: Branford, 1970. 192p. [C]

This British instructor's modern approach to canvaswork emphasizes the striking effects to be achieved for practical and decorative items through the selective use of varied stitches, textures, and colors. Also discussed are design sources and adaptations, transfer techniques, materials, and equipment. Many photographs, some in color, illustrate the innovative techniques for canvaswork, supplemented with straw, glass, and other components to break the monotony. For the more experienced needleworker.

359 ● Rhodes, Mary. Needlepaint; The Art of Canvas Embroidery. London: Octopus, 1974. 144p. [D]

This book not only provides the essential basic information about needlepoint but also emphasizes the creative aspects. The chapter on design, color, and texture will inspire the reader to find shapes and colors in order to express individual ideas. Rhodes presents a short historical survey of the craft and a fully illustrated dictionary of stitches. Over 200 black-and-white illustrations make this book useful for both beginners and more experienced needleworkers.

360 ● Risley, Christine. The Technique of Creative Embroidery. London: Studio Vista; New York: Watson-Guptill, 1971 (© 1969). 96p. [D]

From original design to finished creation, the reader is instructed in each step of the embroidery process, both traditional and experimental. Basic techniques are explained in detail, and stitches are described and illustrated. The projects presented here include pictures, articles of clothing, and household items. The designs are all modern in style and use a great variety of materials, giving inspiration to the reader for further experimentation.

361 ● Rogers, Gay Ann. Tribal Designs for Needlepoint: 30 Original Designs Adapted from Eskimo, Polynesian and Indian Art. Garden City, N.Y.: Doubleday, 1977. 159p. [C]

A nice collection of needlepoint projects based on

tribal art. The designs are all illustrated with graphs, black-and-white drawings, and color photographs. The projects include pillows, pictures, belts, wall hangings, and other items suitable for needlepoint decoration. Since the charts are not always clear, only those with experience should try the designs. A glossary of stitches is appended.

362 ● Rome, Carol Cheney. A New Look at Bargello; The Florentine Needlepoint Stitch book. New York: Crown, 1973. 80p. [B]

Using the terms "Florentine embroidery" and "bargello" interchangeably, the author gives illustrations of traditional patterns and traces the history of this stitch. She details seven basic bargello stitches and gives instructions on how to create individual shapes and colors. These instructions are accompanied by diagrams and photographs, many in color. Four full-size diagrams of animal patterns supplement the usual geometric designs of the traditional bargello embroidery.

363 ● Rome, Carol Cheney, and Georgia French Devlin. A New Look at Needlepoint. New York: Crown, 1972. 229p. [D]

After a brief history of canvas embroidery, the authors give practical instructions for twenty-three projects described in this book. Eighty stitches are presented with detailed suggestions for color, measurements, blocking, and finishing. The projects include personal accessories, gifts, decorative items, and many more. A photograph of each stitch shows how it looks in a finished square. The stitch is also shown with diagrams to enable the user to learn the technique. A rich source of creative designs and beautiful projects.

364 ● Rome, Carol Cheney, and Donna Reidy Orr. Needlepoint Letters and Numbers. New York: Doubleday, 1977. 160p. [B]

Two needlepoint designers suggest interesting creations using letters and numbers. They present twenty-four alphabets and numbers from such unusual sources as International Numeral Pennants and the International Morse Code. The directions include graphs, canvas measurements, photo-

graphs, and the usual technical instructions on how to finish
each project.

365 ● Rosen, Ike. Modern Embroidery. New York: Scribner, 1972. 159p. [D]

Over fifty embroidery designs are presented here,
suitable for both beginners and the experienced. The projects are accompanied by line drawings and photographs,
many in color. These modern designs are adapted to different gift items, such as tablecloths, pillows, and chair
covers. An attempt to enhance a traditional craft with modern elements.

366 ● Rosenstiel, Helena Von. American Rugs and Carpets;
From the 17th Century to Modern Times. New
York: Morrow, 1978. 192p.

A historical survey of rugs, carpets, and other
coverings that have been used in America from Colonial to
modern times. The book starts with straw matting, describing the weaving techniques of the Navajo and other Indian tribes. A full chapter is devoted to the development
of the American carpet industry. Besides the commercially
produced rugs, the author discusses the history and development of handmade rugs done in needlepoint, embroidery, or
hooked techniques. Richly illustrated with full-color and
black-and-white photographs showing pieces, techniques, portraits, and museum pieces, this is an original work with information hard to find anywhere else.

367 ● Ross, Robert Horace. Treasures of Tutankhamun in
Needlepoint. Photographs by Edward L. Wintring-
ham. New York: Morrow, 1978. 86p. [C]

Inspired by the touring museum exhibit of the treasures found in King Tut's tomb and presented to the American
public during 1978-1979. The extraordinary geometric style
of the Egyptian designs adapts itself easily to canvaswork.
The author chose not to transfer the exact images to needle-
work--except the Royal Mask--but rather create original com-
positions with Egyptian motifs. The designs can be used for
borders and frames, but mostly for pillows. Charts and
color-keys are supplied. Because of the elaborate designs,
only experienced needleworkers should try these patterns.

368 ● Rosse, Alianora. Flower Embroidery. New York: Scribner, 1975. 84p. [D]

Flowers--including roses, peonies, tulips, forget-me-nots, daisies, and many wildflowers--have been adapted by the author from bouquets, pictures, and gardens. The seventeen original patterns use a variety of stitches and yarns, and they are adapted for use on a wide range of items, such as tablecloth, pillow, chair, seat cover, purse, pincushion, and hangings. General directions are given, with brief descriptions and indication of materials. There are many sketches and photographs (those in color show the finished pieces). Patterns and color charts for three designs are included. A list at the back of the book gives the common name and the botanical name of each flower.

369 ● Roth, Ann. America in Cross-Stitch. Englewood Cliffs, N.J.: Prentice-Hall, 1976. 111p. [D]

Twenty-one traditional American designs are translated into cross-stitch, using either wool or silk yarns. The author supplies clear, easy-to-follow graphs, instructions, and many illustrations (some in color). The border designs, alphabets, and numbers make this book a useful volume for those who prefer cross-stitch for their needlework.

370 ● Roth, Ann. Mosaic Masterpieces in Needlework and Handicraft Based on Motifs from the Holy Land. New York: Scribner, 1975. 63p. [C]

371 ● Roth, Ann. Needlepoint Desgins from the Mosaics of Ravenna. New York: Scribner, 1975. 63p. [C]

The treatment of the subject and organization in both books follow a similar pattern. First, the author presents the history of the particular region's art, followed by the designs, each accompanied by a black-and-white photograph of the original and a color plate of the finished project. The author takes these designs from ancient Italian and Israeli churches, synagogues, and other historical monuments. The designs are clear and easy to follow, but because of their complexity much experience is needed for their execution. Included are general instructions and explanations of the different techniques. The designs are mostly geometrics or animal forms, with a few religious objects.

109

372 ● Ruffini-Parolini, Elvira. Charted Swiss Folk Designs. New York: Dover, 1980. 32p. [B]

The book presents a collection of over 100 charted designs from the Engadine Valley of Switzerland. These central and border designs are easily adaptable to cross-stitch, needlepoint, or rug-hooking. The patterns include flowers, animals, hunting scenes, and so on. With short instructions, the book is a useful source of ideas for more experienced needleworkers.

373 ● Rush, Beverly. Stitch with Style. Seattle: Madrona, 1979. 92p. [C]

The author discusses various types of embroidery, as applied to garments and other useful objects, such as tablecloths and linens. They include both modern and traditional designs. The illustrations are mostly in black-and-white, but some are in color. A substantial part of the book deals with materials, marking methods, making the garment, and special fabrics. Some of the designs are shown on graphs. Enclosed is a glossary of stitches. A rich collection of unusual designs and their adaptations. Only for the more experienced needleworker.

374 ● Rush, Beverly. The Stitchery Idea Book. New York: Van Nostrand, 1974. 176p. [C]

A wealth of ideas for something more ambitious than the usual sampler, with over 300 black-and-white photographs, each accompanied by explanations of methods, materials, and diagrams, when necessary. The book does not waste space on basic techniques but emphasizes design elements, and how to teach, learn, and exhibit stitchery. The methods discussed cover not only embroidery but appliqué, trapunto, patchwork, needle lace, and other techniques. A glossary and an index of techniques complete this useful volume.

375 ● Russell, Pat. Lettering for Embroidery. London: Batsford; New York: Van Nostrand, 1971. 160p. [B]

The book addresses the art of lettering in various forms of needlework. The author begins with the basic design of the alphabet, then proceeds to show and explain lettering in many needlework techniques, such as appliqué, crewel, cross-stitch, and needlepoint. A wealth of illustrations show both modern and old examples, from Roman times to the present. Illuminated manuscripts, religious articles with letters, handkerchiefs, and many other possible applications are presented here, in great variety. The last chapter is a glossary of alphabets. An unusual, interesting book on lettering, with countless forms and materials for further application.

376 ● Sara, Dorothy. The Key to Crewel Embroidery; The Gracious Embroidery for Interior Decorating and Personal Items. New York: Paddel, 1972 © 1966). 82p. [A]

Following an introductory chapter on materials, fabrics, yarns, framing, and so on, the author presents twenty-five basic stitches and a collection of samplers, showing the practical applications of the stitches. After presenting a few designs, she gives instructions on how to make and apply designs on your own. Illustrations are only in black-and-white. A basic book, useful mostly for the stitches, because the designs are poor and are poorly illustrated.

377 ● Sara, Dorothy. The Key to Needlepoint; The Timeless Art of Needlepoint on Canvas for Home and Personal Accessories. New York: Paddel, 1972 © 1967). 73p. [A]

This is a short guide to the basic techniques of needlepoint, including materials, yarns, stitches, and so on. The author encourages readers to create their own designs. Illustrations, in black-and-white, are of poor quality. The practical hints are useful, however, and the stitches are clearly explained. Not a workbook, but a guide to the basics of needlepoint.

378 ● Sayles, Shirley. Step-by-Step Stitchery. New York: Golden Press, 1976. 80p. [C]

This volume gives good technical instructions for a great variety of patterns. The designs include both traditional and modern styles. The technique is mostly embroidery, with a few designs in needlepoint. A good work-book with many unusual designs. Since the patterns are quite intricate, with unusual stitches and techniques, the book is suitable for more experienced needleworkers.

379 ● Scheuer, Nikki. Designs for Holbein Embroidery: 110 New Geometric Patterns. Garden City, N.Y.: Doubleday, 1976. 136p. [C]

Holbein embroidery (more commonly known as blackwork) is a form of counted-thread embroidery applied with black yarn on white fabric. The author presents in this volume twenty-five designs and projects and more than 100 patterns. A brief introduction describes the basic tech-niques, and the good illustrations make it easier for the user to copy the patterns. A list of suppliers and a bibli-ography are appended.

380 ● Schiffer, Margaret B. Historical Needlework of Penn-sylvania. New York: Scribner, 1968. 160p. [D]

This book covers various styles in needlework, in particular the styles of the early settlers in Pennsylvania-- the Quakers, the Moravians, and the Pennsylvania "Dutch." More than 100 examples are described and illustrated in this volume. Almost half of them are samplers worked by schoolgirls and preserved in still-existing schools, notably that at Westtown, or by the families. The pieces, done in darning, cross-stitch, crewel embroidery, Florentine stitch (bargello), and canvaswork (needlepoint), are both simple and sophisticated, and can be adapted to many uses.

381 ● Schnitzer, Jeanne, and Ginny Ross. New Dimensions in Needlework. Englewood Cliffs, N.J.: Prentice-Hall, 1977. 178p. [C]

Beginning with a brief history of the craft, the author presents technical instructions and a collection of beautiful, original designs. The designs are applied to a great variety of articles, such as dinner jacket, fur-trimmed coat, rugs with Persian motifs, and pillows. The styles are mixed, some Oriental, others traditional or modern. The finished articles are illustrated in color photographs. An unusual workbook, but only for the more experienced.

382 ● Schraffenberger, Nancy, ed. Woman's Day Decorative
Needlework for the Home. New York: Columbia
House; dist. by Sterling, 1981. 176p. [D]

This collection of reprints from Woman's Day magazine covers various types of needlework, among them needlepoint, crochet, and embroidery. The user can find a
wide range of projects, including pillows, pictures, wall
hangings, and afghans. The illustrations are clear, with
step-by-step directions and photographs, some in color.
Styles are mostly traditional, appealing to the tastes of today's American homes.

383 ● Scobey, Joan. Rugs and Wall Hangings; Period Designs and Contemporary Techniques. Original designs and illustrations by Majorie Sablow. New
York: Dial, 1974. 244p. [C]

The first part of this book is devoted to the history of rugs; how rug design originated, how rugmaking traditions started, what the materials and techniques were.
The second part is a workbook, giving instructions on how
to design and make a rug. The techniques include needlepoint, latch-hooking, punch-needle, and rya. Many beautiful illustrations (in both color and black-and-white) of original designs or museum pieces are presented. At the end
of the volume, about thirty designs are shown on graph paper for easy copying. Not the usual how-to book, but rather
a historical essay with a very comprehensive treatment of
rugmaking. The intricate Oriental designs should be attempted only by the experienced.

384 ● Scobey, Joan, and Lee Parr McGraft. Celebrity Needlepoint. New York: Dial, 1972. 166p. [D]

The authors collected many types of needlework
done by American celebrities today. The collection includes
pillows, tabletops, chair coverings, and so on. Most of the
celebrities--there are men as well as women--come from
the fields of entertainment and the arts, but they represent
sports, politics, and business as well. In personal inter-
views, they tell all about why, where, and how they started
their needlepoint hobby. Illustrations, many in color, show
the celebrities' creations. A special section deals with the
basic needlepoint techniques and includes a variety of stitches,

color schemes, finishing, and so on. An unusual how-to
book with inspiration for further experimentation.

385 ● Scobey, Joan, and Marjorie Sablow. Decorating with
      Needlepoint. Des Moines: Meredith, 1975. 192p.
      [B]

      A useful workbook for home-decorating projects
using needlepoint. Forty-two projects are presented, including chair cover, piano bench, serving tray, card table,
and rug. Each project is described separately, with the
necessary basic instructions, graphs, special tips for work,
and finishing instructions. A color photograph of the finished product appears in each part.

386 ● Scobey, Joan, and Lee Parr McGrath. Do-It-All-
      Yourself Needlepoint. Original designs by Mar-
      jorie Sablow. Photographs by Eugene Sablow. New
      York: Simon and Schuster, 1971. 184p. [C]

      The authors offer the reader an alternative for the
ready-made painted canvas. They include all the practical
details on how to create a needlework project from start to
finish. They give instructions for specific projects, which
are illustrated with black-and-white photographs. Fifty-eight
pages of patterns on graph paper are appended for easy copying. The lack of color photographs greatly reduces the book's
attractiveness.

387 ● Scobey, Joan, and Marjorie Sablow. The First Easy-
      to-See Needlepoint Workbook. New York: Rawson,
      1977. 193p. [B]

      Everything about this book is oversized, including
the pages and the type. Thirty original projects are scaled
specifically for large-mesh canvases (#5, #7, and #10 mesh
to the inch). The projects are varied--accessories, pillows,
hangings, and so on. After the first chapter, which discusses supplies and techniques, the projects are described
with detailed instructions and illustrated with charts and
drawings. The finished products, shown on color plates,
are very attractive. The last chapter is a design workbook
with letters and numbers. The oversized charts make this
book easy to work with, even for those with some difficulty
in vision.

388 ● Scobey, Joan, and Marjorie Sablow. Rugmaking: 3
Quick and Easy Ways. Indianapolis: Bobbs-Merrill, 1977. 136p. [D]

Three techniques to make beautiful rugs--needle-
point, latch-hook, and punch-hook--are discussed in this
book. Original rug designs are presented in three color
schemes, each with a corresponding working design. For
each technique, the necessary instructions are given, with
practical advice for blocking, finishing, fringes, and other
matters. A useful workbook for those who would like to
create their own rugs. The level of difficulty ranges from
simple to complicated.

389 ● The Scribner Book of Embroidery Design. Edited by
Muriel Baker. New York: Scribner, 1980. 152p.
[C]

The title of this book is misleading, since the type
of needlework presented here includes, besides embroidery,
a variety of other techniques, such as bargello, blackwork,
and needlepoint. The editor collected thirty-six patterns
from nineteen designers. Each design is accompanied by
complete instructions, graphs, and photographs of the finished product. For the more experienced needleworker.

390 ● Searls, Maxine. Basic Needlepoint. New York:
Galahad, 1972. 87p. [A]

This volume shows clearly and simply all the basic
needlepoint techniques. The projects are simple, with good
explanations, charts, and color keys. They include a great
variety of items, such as rugs, throw pillows, belts, purses,
pincushions, handbags, and hangings. A useful book for both
beginners and the more experienced.

391 ● Sebba, Anne. Samplers; Five Centuries of a Gentle
Craft. London: Thames and Hudson; dist. by
Norton, 1979. 151p. [C]

A rich collection of samplers from Europe and
America, illustrated with black-and-white and color photographs. The author surveys the historical development of
samplers, providing illustrations of many samplers from

various periods. Since there are no graphs or detailed patterns in this book, it will be used only by more experienced needleworkers.

392 ● Short, Eirian. Embroidery and Fabric Collage. New York: Scribner, 1967. 130p. [C]

The term "embroidery" is used in the widest sense in this book, which explores the possibilities of the medium, particularly in view of the rapid development of modern principles of design. It is aimed at those who are experienced in all types of needlework and are looking for new avenues. The book presents patterns and designs (mostly in black-and-white) that can be used for original, imaginative work, and a great variety of projects. Several museum pieces are also illustrated. The projects comprise a great variety of articles, such as dresses, household items, and so on. The author encourages readers to use embroidery as a medium of artistic expression.

393 ● Sibbett, Ed, Jr. Peasant Designs for Artists and Craftsmen. New York: Dover, 1977. 112p. [D]

This book contains a large collection of authentic Central and Eastern European folk motifs. Some 255 illustrations include florals, animals, birds, human figures in folk costumes, borders, frames, and corners. Each can be used as a single design or can be combined into larger pieces. The motifs are best suited for embroidery, using a variety of stitches, or for stencilwork. Technical instructions are not included, leaving the actual execution of the work to the creative ability of the user.

394 ● Sidney, Sylvia. Question and Answer Book on Needlepoint. New York: Van Nostrand, 1974. 128p. [B]

The author, an actress and expert needlewoman, wrote this book "on popular demand" to answer questions most often "not fully answered in many needlecraft and embroidery books." The questions discussed refer mostly to design, selection of materials, and finishing the project. Color and black-and-white illustrations accompany each chapter. A final chapter covers various stitches, providing easy instructions and black-and-white illustrations.

395 ● Sidney, Sylvia. Sylvia Sidney's Needlepoint Book.
New York: Galahad, 1968. 120p. [D]

A thorough, comprehensive book about all aspects
of needlepoint, enhanced by the author's personal style, practical advice, and beautiful original designs. Sylvia Sidney
is not only an actress but a serious needlewoman whose
works have been highly praised by professionals. The book
has been written primarily for those who know something
about needlework but want to go on to more expressive techniques. It is clearly presented, with plenty of photographs,
charts, and drawings. Both beginners and the more experienced can use this volume as a workbook or as a complete
guide.

396 ● Siegler, Susan. Needlework Patterns from the Metro-
politan Museum of Art. New York: New York
Graphic Society, 1976. 184p. [C]

Siegler has adapted for embroidery and needlepoint
canvas twenty-four designs based on art owned by the Metro-
politan. The designs span many countries and periods. Each
pattern, illustrated in color and in black-and-white, is fur-
nished with complete directions, including yarn, color, materials, and so on. Only for experienced needleworkers.

397 ● Silverstein, Mira. Bargello Plus. New York: Scribner, 1973. 90p. [C]

Not a basic book on bargello (Florentine embroidery, flame stitch, or Hungarian stitch), this volume does,
however, offer unusual applications. The stitch is combined
with other needlepoint stitches--continental, basket weave,
and so on. Flowers, animals, scenes, and borders are presented with graphs and full information about the techniques
and materials. A rich source of original designs.

398 ● Silverstein, Mira. Fun with Bargello. New York:
Scribner, 1971. 48p. [A]

This compact, easy-to-follow guide for the beginner, specifically in bargello, provides step-by-step directions, with photographs and diagrams. Some possible variations for the designs, and instructions on how to calculate
the amount of yarn for each project, are included.

399 ● Silverstein, Mira. Guide to Slanted Stitches; Exciting
Needlework Projects, Patterns and Designs Anyone
Can Make. New York: McKay, 1977. 128p. [C]

In this good workbook, with many original patterns
for the experienced needleworker, the description and illus-
tration of stitches occupy about forty pages. The rest of
the volume is devoted to patterns and projects. They are
shown on graphs for easy copying, and the finished products
are illustrated in color photographs.

400 ● Silverstein, Mira. International Needlework Designs.
Artwork by Roberta Frauwirth; photographs by
Sandy L. Studios. New York: Scribner, 1978.
180p. [C]

Here is a rich collection of needlework samples
from various sources, such as museums, private collections,
and so forth. The directions, although complete, could be
best used by experienced needleworkers. Not only needlepoint, but appliqué, trapunto, blackwork, and many other
techniques are covered. The different stitches are presented
with detailed description and illustrations. A list of suppliers and bibliography is appended.

401 ● Silverstein, Mira. Mira Silverstein's Guide to Combination Stitches. Artwork by Roberta Frauwirth;
photographs by Sandy L. Studios. New York: Mc-
Kay, 1977. 120p. [C]

The author offers in this book original projects
that use a combination of stitches, such as needlepoint, bargello, or embroidery. After the technical instructions, the
patterns and projects are presented with easy-to-follow descriptions, charts, and color plates. An attractive workbook
with beautiful designs that utilize an unusual combination of
stitches.

402 ● Silverstein, Mira. Mira Silverstein's Guide to Looped
and Knotted Stitches. Artwork by Roberta Frauwirth; photographs by Sandy L. Studios. New York:
McKay, 1977. 107p. [C]

Similar in arrangement to the author's other books,
this volume presents original designs worked mostly in looped

or knotted stitches. In the instructions, the author puts special emphasis on those stitches and their applications. The patterns and projects are set out with clear descriptions, charts, and color plates. A good workbook for these stitches and their unusual applications.

403 ● Simmons, Sue, ed. Creative Rugmaking. Chicago: Regnery, 1976. 88p. [D]

This book shows the reader how to make unusual rugs, using a combination of skills and materials. From latch-hook to needlepoint, many techniques are demonstrated in a variety of patterns--Turkish, Scandinavian, modern, and so on. Instructions are clear, with diagrams and illustrations. A collection of beautiful projects, giving inspiration for further design possibilities.

404 ● Simpson, Jane. The Basic Book of Embroidery. London: Octopus, 1973. 128p. [A]

An introduction to the basic stitches of embroidery. The author, in fully illustrated instructions, shows how to do the basic stitches and explains the techniques of transferring designs from paper to material and finishing the work. The book contains twenty-four designs, with charts, color pictures, and practical applications, such as dress, apron, wall panel, and needlework bag.

405 ● Simpson, Jane. The Color Book of Embroidery. Secaucus, N.J.: Chartwell, 1977. 91p. [A]

Basic embroidery stitches are explained and illustrated, with clear descriptions and photographs of the finished projects. The stitches and samples include not only embroidery, but patchwork, quilting, appliqué, and smocking. A good basic book for beginners.

406 ● Simpson, Jean. Shisha Mirror Embroidery; A Contemporary Approach. Photographs by Don Rasmussen; illustrations by Gwenn Stutzman. New York: Van Nostrand, 1978. 104p. [C]

Shisha mirror embroidery is a needlework technique

that involves stitching shisha ("little glass") mirrors in a framework of other embroidery stitches. Developed in India three centuries ago, it can transform clothes, accessories, or toys into sparkling, individualized creations. The author provides step-by-step instructions for ten basic stitching procedures. She also describes different kinds of shisha mirrors, fabrics, threads, and equipment. A large collection of practical applications are presented with drawings and photographs, some in color. A complete book for an unusual type of embroidery, requiring some previous experience in needlework.

407 ● Slater, Elaine. Elaine Slater's Book of Needlepoint Projects. Illustrated by Lisa Levitt. New York: Holt, 1978. 190p. [D]

Slater divided this book into four parts: first, working from a painted canvas; second, tracing your own design; third, working on blank canvas; fourth, working from a graph. The book opens with an extensive question-and-answer chapter, followed by an illustrated section about stitches. All the techniques are described in detail, with line drawings. Eight pages in full color show the finished products. A comprehensive, easy-to-use workbook about all aspects of needlepoint, with attractive projects.

408 ● Slater, Elaine. The New York Times Book of Needlepoint. New York: Quadrangle, 1973. 247p. [D]

The author presents a step-by-step manual with color illustrations and diagrams. She describes ten basic techniques for beginners and provides more difficult designs for advanced needleworkers. She explains the materials needed, as well as the techniques for blocking and finishing. Illustrations include such varied uses of needlepoint as wall hangings, totebags, and letters of the alphabet.

409 ● Slater, Elaine. The New York Times Book of Needlepoint for Left-handers. New York: Quadrangle, 1974. 247p. [D]

Following the style and format of her earlier volume, Slater created a manual specifically for left-handed people. The stitches are fully illustrated for left-handers, progressing from simple to more complicated projects. The author uses samplers to familiarize the user with each stitch. Both the illustrations and the photographs of the finished projects are presented in color. A necessary volume for left-handed needleworkers.

410 ● Smith, Glenora. Needlery: The Connoisseur's Album of Adventures in Needlepoint and Embroidery. New York: Butterick, 1978. 208p. [D]

The author combines needlepoint and embroidery into one craft--needlery--and provides twenty-six designs for her innovative technique. For each design, color photograph, charts, stitch types, and special instructions are provided. The appendix lists needlework schools, collections, and suppliers. With a bibliography.

411 ● Snook, Barbara. The Creative Art of Embroidery. London, New York: Hamlyn, 1972. 176p. [D]

The basic techniques and principal categories of embroidery are presented in this book. A well-illustrated dictionary of embroidery stitches gives clear working instructions. The first chapter covers the history of embroidery, discussing separately the special features for various nations. Over twenty designs are presented with diagrams, drawings, and other illustrations, partially in color. The designs include pillows, pictures, pillow cases, motifs for dresses, and so on. A rich source of embroidery designs for various applications.

412 ● Snook, Barbara L. Embroidery Designs from Pre-Columbian Art. New York: Scribner, 1975. 134p. [C]

The designs in this book have been adapted from Aztec, Mayan, and Inca pottery, baskets, and textiles. Some are abstract; others show strange birds, animals, serpents, and fish. Adaptable to both crewel and needlepoint techniques, they can be used as decorative elements on many items, such as cushions, curtains, linens, shirts, and skirts. The designs are illustrated with drawings; and stitches and colors are marked. A workbook with unusual patterns for

the more experienced needleworker, since some of the designs are quite complicated.

413 ● Snook, Barbara. Embroidery Designs from the Sea.
       New York: Taplinger, 1977. 96p. [C]

     Snook uses the sea as an inspiration for embroi-
dery designs. The animals of the sea--octopus, jellyfish,
crab, seahorse, and others--are represented in the designs,
complemented with patterns inspired by marine flora. The
designs are well illustrated and accompanied by technical instructions. This book is a source of unusual patterns for
the experienced needleworker.

414 ● Snook, Barbara. Florentine Embroidery. New York:
       Scribner, 1967. 160p. [B]

     The book deals with Florentine embroidery, some-
times called flame stitch, Hungarian point, and, more recently, bargello. The stitch lends itself to a great variety
of uses, such as wall hangings, rugs, seat covers, pillows,
handbags, and small accessories. The author gives diagrams for thirty-three variations of the stitch and instructions for twenty-one articles. Also included is general
practical advice about colors, blocking, and finishing. Anyone who enjoys working with a needle will find this kind of
embroidery a fascinating recreation and art.

415 ● Sorensen, Grethe. Needlepoint Designs from Oriental
       Rugs. New York: Scribner, 1981. 90p. [C]

     This book contains the usual introduction and his-
torical background, and also chapters on materials, blocking, and finishing. The unusual part of the book are the
fifteen patterns, which the author adapted from Turkish, Persian, and Caucasian rugs. These patterns are ready to be
copied with the help of charts, and the finished products are
shown in photographs, some of them in color. Color charts
and yarn quantities are provided. Beautiful, but very intricate, patterns for experienced needleworkers.

416 ● Spence, Anne. Creative Embroidery; A Complete
       Guide. New York: Viking, 1975. 152p. [C]

The book explores hand stitchery and simple machine stitchery, providing a full and practical account, from
preparatory work to completion, of the many effects that can
be achieved with needlework. Ten methods--embroidery,
quilting, appliqué, cutwork, drawn and pulled threadwork,
among others--are explained and illustrated. The emphasis
is on creativity throughout, and a separate chapter on design encourages experiments with shape, color, and texture.
A final chapter on allied crafts, such as weaving on a frame
loom, tie dye, and batik, suggests how these can be used
in conjunction with stitchery to extend creative embroidery
far beyond its usual confines. The text is complemented by
full-color plates and black-and-white drawings and photographs.

417 ● Springall, Diana. Canvas Embroidery. Newton Centre, Mass.: Branford, 1969. 129p. [B]

This rich source of inspiration for canvas embroidery (needlepoint) provides clear, easy-to-follow instructions
for sample stitches, accompanied by photographs, some in
color. There is ample technical advice as to shape, color,
stitches, yarn, and individualized effect for each piece.

418 ● Springer, Jo. Creative Needlework. Designed by
Solweig Hedin. Edited by Edith Noonberg. New
York: Westport, 1974. 256p. [D]

An enlarged version, very similar in arrangement
and treatment of the subject (although wider in scope), of
Springer's earlier book, published in 1969 under the same
title. An unusual feature of the book is that patterns for
little-practiced types of needlework, such as metal stumpwork, appliqué, and darnwork, are included. The expanded
edition, using the same samples and photographs as in the
earlier edition, contains an added chapter, entitled "Boutique" with more designs for pillows, hats, belts, scarves,
and other accessories.

419 ● Springer, Jo. Pleasures of Crewel. New York:
Universal; dist. by Springer, 1972. 166p. [D]

This excellent and comprehensive book about all
aspects of crewel embroidery covers history, basic stitches,

yarns, colors, and materials. Projects are grouped according to experience. Professional finishing tips and decorating ideas make this book a useful addition to the shelf of embroidery books.

420 ● Stearns, Martha Genung. Homespun and Blue; A Study of American Crewel Embroidery. New York: Scribner, 1963. 96p.

The author tells the story of early American embroidery, which will be of interest to collectors, students of Americana, and the many people who are doing crewel embroidery today. Much of the history of New England and Colonial times is reflected in the samplers, rugs, and curtains described and illustrated in this book.

421 ● Stevens, Gigs. Free-form Bargello. New York: Scribner, 1977. 106p. [C]

This volume presents a modern variation on classic bargello, or Florentine, embroidery. Disregarding the old rule of bargello, Stevens uses the long upright stitch in pictorial designs and impressionistic patterns. The author explains how to start such a project with a central motif, either abstract or pictorial, then enlarge it with successive "waves" according to one's fancy. She points out that this technique is particularly effective for large pieces, such as rugs and wall hangings.

422 ● Story, Dorothy P. Full-Color American Indian Designs for Needlepoint Rugs; Charted for Easy Use. New York: Dover, 1975. 35p. [A]

Story adapted the thirty-two motifs in this book from a wide variety of authentic artworks of the Plains and Southwestern Indian tribes. She feels that the boldness of these designs makes them particularly appropriate for large needlepoint pieces. She has therefore charted them for easy use on #5 rug canvas. However, the designs can also be executed on small-gauge canvas, in which case the finished work is smaller and more compact. These charted designs will also be useful in many other forms of needlework, such as rug hooking and cross-stitch embroidery.

423 ● Sumner, Mary, Helen Wilson, and Claire Deutsch.
    Basic Needlepoint.   New York: Harper, 1971.
    32p. [A]

     A basic guide for beginners, without patterns or
projects.   Only the stitches are presented here, with large,
easy-to-follow diagrams and basic technical instruction on
material, yarn, color, blocking, and mounting.   The stitches
are also shown and explained for left-handed people.   A
basic book for young people or beginners.

424 ● Sunset.   Needlepoint.   By the editors of Sunset Books
    and Sunset magazine.   Menlo Park, Calif.: Lane,
    1972.   80p. [A]

     A good introduction to basic needlepoint stitches,
with clear drawings, charts, and color pictures of the finished products.   The technical instructions are sufficient
and clear.   The simple projects make it possible for the
beginner to learn the basic techniques of needlepoint.

425 ● Sunset.   Needlepoint Techniques and Projects.   By
    the editors of Sunset Books.   Menlo Park, Calif.:
    Lane, 1977.   80p. [B]

     Keeping in tradition with other Sunset books, this
volume is a compact guide to needlepoint.   Stitches are presented on graph paper and in photographs for easy understanding.   The projects are shown in detail (in color) with
all the necessary technical and finishing instructions.   The
projects are attractive and can be done with little experience.

426 ● Sunset.   Stitchery, Embroidery, Appliqué, Crewel.
    By the editors of Sunset Books.   Menlo Park,
    Calif.: Lane, 1974.   80p. [C]

     The book covers a variety of techniques, with in-
structions, diagrams, and a glossary of stitches.   The projects range from simple to the more sophisticated.   The patterns are modernistic in style, using bold, bright colors.
These original designs are fully explained and are illustrated
with drawings and full-color photographs.   The technical instructions are short but sufficient.   The book tries to pack
a great amount of information into a relatively small space.

Since basic instructions are kept to a minimum, this is only
for the more experienced needleworkers.

427 ● Svennas, Elsie.   A Handbook of Lettering for Stitchers.
      New York: Van Nostrand, 1973. 92p. [D]

The author first presents a concise history of lettering, tracing its development from the simplest markings
to elaborate monograms.   The book contains an illustrated
dictionary of all stitches, suitable for lettering.   Finally,
Svennas illustrates the alphabet with many stitches, including possible combinations of letters for monograms.   The
book will appeal to those who are interested in embroidery
and enjoy monogramming.

428 ● Swain, Margaret.   The Needlework of Mary, Queen
      of Scots.   New York: Van Nostrand, 1973.
      128p.

This book is the first comprehensive study of the
Queen of Scots as a needlewoman, describing all surviving
works associated with her.   As an understanding of her work
would be difficult without some reference to her life, a brief
biographical outline provides a framework for the book.   The
author tries to explain what role needlework played in her
life, an absorbing pastime in her years of imprisonment.
Mary's pieces are presented in photographs, some in color,
mostly from museums in Great Britain.   An interesting work
in the history of costume and textiles, and a new and interesting aspect of Queen Mary's life.

429 ● Swan, Susan Burrows.   Plain and Fancy; American
      Women and Their Needlework.   New York: Holt,
      1977.   240p. [C]

This book not only provides the user with the history of American needlework in the eighteenth and early nineteenth centuries, but surveys, as a background, the history
of American women during this period.   More than 150 photographs (some in color) are taken from the Henry Francis Du Pont Winterthur Museum in Delaware.   The most representative among the needlework is the "Irish stitch"--what
we today call bargello.   Besides the Irish stitch, many pieces
are worked in needlepoint, cross-stitch, crewel embroidery,

appliqué, and other techniques. This book is not the usual how-to volume but rather an essay on early American needlework and a social history of American women.

430 ● Szalavary, Anne. Hungarian Folk Designs for Embroiderers and Craftsmen. New York: Dover, 1977. 128p. [D]

For centuries, Hungarian craftsworkers have practiced decorating furniture, walls, and pottery with regional motifs, peculiar to numerous ethnic and geographical areas. This book presents over 250 designs, chiefly florals, with instructions for transferring into fabrics. The designs are applicable to different types of needlework, but mostly for embroidery and needlepoint. This is not a workbook but rather a rich collection of beautiful designs for the use of the more experienced needleworker or for other craftspeople.

431 ● Thomas, Mary. Mary Thomas' Embroidery Book. New York: Gramercy, 1937. 304p. [D]

This reprint of a classic in its field is a practical guide to many embroidery stitches, similar to the author's Dictionary of Needlework Stitches. The author clearly shows how to combine a variety of stitches into different patterns. The illustrations are only in black-and-white but contain patterns and stitches not to be found in the more recent publications. Useful either as a workbook or as a reference guide.

432 ● Thompson, Ginnie. Favorite Illustrations from Children's Classics in Counted Cross-Stitch. New York: Dover, 1980. 42p. [B]

The book presents twenty-eight designs based on the work of famous illustrators for children's classics--e.g., Tenniel's illustrations for Alice in Wonderland, Denslow's for The Wizard of Oz, and Kate Greenaway's for other children's stories. The designs are charted for cross-stitch but can be adapted to needlepoint. Basic, short instructions are included with charts and color-keys. Some experience is necessary for the execution of the designs.

433 ● Thorne-Thomsen, Kathleen. Alice in Stitches. New York: Holt, 1979. 96p. [D]

More than thirty original needlepoint patterns are presented in this book, inspired by the classic story Alice in Wonderland. Using the same format as Mother Goose in Stitches (see below), the author offers easy-to-follow instructions, basic projects, and original designs. She completely covers the basics of both techniques (cross-stitch and needlepoint), making the book useful for both beginners and the more experienced. Ten color plates, illustrating the finished projects, appear at the end of the volume.

434 ● Thorne-Thomsen, Kathleen. Mother Goose in Stitches. New York: Holt, 1976. 96p. [A]

More than forty needlework projects are presented in this volume, designed by the author and creating such wonderful Mother Goose characters as Humpty Dumpty and Peter Pumpkin Eater. The directions are clear and easy-to-follow; they include graphs, suggested techniques, applications, finishing, and so on. A list of suppliers is appended.

435 ● Thorne-Thomsen, Kathleen, and Hildy Page Burns. American Cross-Stitch. New York: Van Nostrand, 1974. 104p. [B]

A collection of patterns inspired by our American heritage, including legends and folklore. Black-and-white charts with color keys are included. The patterns can be adapted for different projects according to the wishes of the user.

436 ● Tillett, Leslie. African Art in Needlework. New York: Crowell, 1979. 143p. [D]

The book offers new designs, for both beginners, and the more experienced, based on African motifs. Forty projects are presented, with sketches of the original artifacts and corresponding graphs. Collected from African motifs in architecture, sculpture, painting, and jewelry, Tillett offers new ideas in design in this artistic journey through Sub-Saharan Africa.

437 ● Tillett, Leslie. American Needlework, 1776/1976; Needlepoint and Crewel Patterns Adapted from His-

toric American Images. Boston: New York Graphic Society, 1975. 144p. [D]

Two centuries of American history are adapted to
needlework in this colorful compendium on the Bicentennial
theme. Twenty-eight charming and amusing patterns are
presented here, such as a piece of Martha Washington needlepoint, a Confederate flag, and an Indian drawing of Cus-
ter. Practical tips and instructions are included. Each design is accompanied by drawings, graphs, color photographs,
and suggestions for alternative colors. The level of difficulty range from the beginner to the more experienced.

438 ● Tillett, Leslie. The Zoophabet Needlework Book; An
Alphabet for Needleworkers. New York: Crowell,
1977. 60p. [C]

The letters of the alphabet are presented here in
unusual designs. Each letter embodies animals and plants
whose names begin with that letter. On the facing page,
each creature is drawn separately--with the drawing numer-
ically coded to a color chart. Instructions are minimal, but
the user is compensated with the designs, which can be used
for many projects. According to the author, they can be
adapted for a variety of techniques, such as embroidery,
needlepoint, or bargello. The book is intended for needleworkers with considerable experience.

439 ● Tod, Osma Gallinger. Wool Stitchery. (Original title:
Embroidery in Wools.) New York: Gramercy,
196? 110p. [C]

This reprint of an older edition presents embroidery stitches in many new ways, such as cross-stitch used
for background, ideas for edges and seams, and decorative
finishes for appliqué. The diagrams are clear and easy to
follow. The lack of color illustrations makes the book less
attractive than other, similar volumes.

440 ● Urban, Sandra. Charted Borders, Bands and Corners.
New York: Dover, 1981. 48p. [C]

This book presents a rich collection of repeating
patterns, designed to be used with such traditional needle-

work items as pillows, clothing, trims, and mirror or picture frames. The designs are charted for ready use in different forms of needlework (needlepoint, latch-hooking, cross-
stitch, crochet) and are meant to be worked continuously until the required space is filled. The singular elements making up each design are easily repeated, making any length or
width feasible--a definite plus when making projects that require an odd shape. The book contains over 100 patterns,
worked on #10 canvas. The author included a short introduction with hints on selecting colors, varying the designs
for interesting effects, and working corner patterns.

441 ● Victorian Alphabets, Monograms, and Names for Needleworkers, from Godey's Lady's Book and Peterson's Magazine. Edited by Rita Weiss. New York:
Dover, 1978. 128p. [B]

A large selection of alphabets are presented in
this book, including initials, monograms, and common names,
selected from the most popular American women's magazines of the Victorian era. Each is available in a variety
of letter forms, such as script, floral, or geometric. These
patterns can be used for traditional embroidery and sewing
needs or can be adapted to modern use--e.g., decorating
blue jeans and hats or making patches. Short instructions
for transferring designs are included.

442 ● Vogue. Vogue Guide to Needlepoint Tapestry. London and Glasgow: Collins, 1974. 80p. [C]

The book is a useful compendium of needlepoint
projects--picture of a house, Oriental carpets, hangings,
backgrounds, pillows, evening bags, chairs, and so on.
Fifty-one needlepoint stitches are described, and arranged
in alphabetical order. Following the stitches are chapters
on the technical aspects of needlework--stretching, finishing,
colors, yarns, etc. The designs are basic, leaving the various applications to the reader. The title is somewhat misleading, since this book deals strictly with needlepoint, not
tapestry. A volume for the more experienced.

443 ● Wall, Maggie. Creative Needlepoint Borders. Drawings by Barbara Eyre; photographs by Harold Pratt.
New York: Scribner, 1977. 107p. [C]

Wall created a number of original borders to "frame" needlepoint pieces or to be used for other projects. She covers several techniques in addition to needlepoint-- e.g., pulled threadwork. Although there are sufficient instructions for the different designs, only experienced needle-workers should attempt them. Blank graphs "to draw your own" are appended.

444 ● Warren, Geoffrey. A Stitch in Time: Victorian and Edwardian Needlecraft. New York: Taplinger, 1976. 144p.

An informative essay on Victorian needlecraft in Great Britain. Although the author emphasizes the over-abundance and often tastelessness of needlecraft in the mid-dle-class British home, he never forgets that much Victorian work is copied and reconstructed today. Illustrations complement the well-written text.

445 ● Weal, Michele. Texture and Color in Needlepoint. New York: Harper, 1975. [C]

The author presents a rich collection of patterns, with step-by-step directions and tips on dimensions, color, stitches, and so on. She goes beyond the simple description of the projects, and provides information on color combinations, a "mini-course" in color fundamentals, and guidelines about how to use needlepoint in interior design. Finally, she gives instructions how to design your own textured needlepoint--the technique emphasized in this book.

446 ● Weaver, Gabrielle, ed. Tapestry and Needlepoint. London, New York: Cavendish, 1976. 88p. [B]

The book begins with an introduction to tapestry and the description of weaving techniques. Weaving occupies only twenty-four pages, however, the rest of the book deals with needlepoint. The various stitches are fully illustrated in color, and the projects presented are mostly simple and practical. Each is given a full description, with charts and color photos of the finished projects.

447 ● Weiss, Rita, ed. Charted Monograms for Needlepoint

and Cross-Stitch.   New York: Dover, 1980.   48p.
[A]

The monogram is a popular form of ornamentation
for tableclothes, napkins, sheets, pillow cases, and many
other items.   This collection gives needleworkers 350 monograms to choose from.   All the monograms that can be composed with pairs of letters are here.   With a little experience, the user is able to copy the charts.   The designs are
adaptable to cross-stitch or needlepoint.

448 ● Weiss, Rita.   Christmas Needlepoint Designs.   New
     York: Dover, 1980.   32p. [B]

Thirty-six Christmas designs are rendered in this
book for easy transfer to #10 needlepoint canvas.   Among
the designs are Christmas tree, Santa, reindeer, and poin-
settias.   The finished product of each design is shown in
full color on the covers.   The designs could be used not
only for needlepoint but also for cross-stitch and latch-hook.
Short directions are included.   A useful book for those with
some experience in needlework.

449 ● Weiss, Rita.   Design and Chart Your Own Needlepoint.
     New York: Dover, 1976.   24, 16p. [B]

According to Weiss, "you don't have to be an artist or designer" to be able to transform favorite pictures,
photographs, or personal themes into needlepoint.   This book
contains twenty-four sheets of translucent art paper, graphed
to correspond to the mesh on #10, #12, and #14 canvas.
This paper, almost essential for charting needlepoint designs, is difficult to obtain in stores.   The author provides
simple but complete instructions on how to choose materials,
plan projects, work with various stitches, enlarge or re-
duce designs, and so on.   Seventeen illustrations and many
examples in color appear on the covers.   Although the author states that beginners without previous artistic or needlepoint experience can produce easy and effective designs, this
type of work does require in most cases some previous experience.

450 ● Weiss, Rita.   Needlepoint Designs After Illustrations
     by Beatrix Potter; Charted for Easy Use.   New
     York: Dover, 1976.   24p. [A]

This collection of twenty-four charted designs is
adapted from four Beatrix Potter books: "The Tale of Peter
Rabbit," "The Tale of Benjamin Bunny," "The Tailor of
Gloucester," and "The Tale of Two Bad Mice." Each has
been charted for easy use on #12 needlepoint canvas but can
be used very easily in counted cross-stitch and other kinds
of counted embroidery. The pieces can serve as delightful
decorations in a children's room. Color photos of the finished works are presented on the inside and outside covers.

451 ● Weiss, Rita, and Carol Belanger Grafton. The Nee-
       dlepoint Alphabet Sampler. New York: Dover,
       1977. 48p. [C]

The authors present thirty-two stitches with simple
instructions, which include easy-to-follow diagrams and photographs of the finished stitch. The stitches are shown in
full color on the twenty-six letters of the alphabet. Readers
can follow this sampler or create their own with various
combinations of stitches. The book contains sixteen color
plates, thirty-two black-and-white photographs, twenty-six
charts, and thirty-two diagrams. A useful book for needle-
pointing the alphabet for many purposes. For intermediate
or advanced needleworkers.

452 ● Weldon's Needlecraft Editors. Crewel Embroidery,
       Old and New. New York: Hearthside, 1963. 96p.
       [D]

This compendium of all types of information on
crewel embroidery, using both American and English sources,
presents 105 variations of crewel embroidery stitches, with
drawings and descriptive instructions. The chapters on English crewel are adapted--with revisions necessary for American use--from the Encyclopaedia of Needlework, published
by Hearthside Press. The illustrative samples are either
museum pieces or original works of modern designers. Not
a workbook, but a source for individual design. The lack
of color photographs greatly decreases the book's appeal.

453 ● White, A. V. Needlecraft for Juniors. London:
       Routledge; Newton Centre, Mass.: Branford, 1960.
       184p. [A]

Written for young beginners, this book sets out to

develop skill in needlecraft by stages, so that by the end of the book students are able to make individual designs and some simple garments for themselves--e.g., mittens, tote-bags, and belts. The designs are simple and easy to copy. The lack of color illustrations reduces the book's attractiveness.

454 ● Whiting, Gertrude. Old-time Tools and Toys of Needlework. New York: Dover, 1971. 357p.

This reprint of a work originally published in 1928 under the title Tools and Toys of Stitchery is a historic treatment of the tools of many types of needlework, including scissors, thimbles, measures, knitting needles, crochet hooks, hoops, rings, frames, and many more. The history is not limited to the American continent but goes back to the origin of the particular tool, wherever it may be (India, China, Africa, etc.). Some of the articles are reprinted from Antiques magazine. A unique treatment of the history and development of needlework tools that features many illustrations, mostly photographs from private collections.

455 ● Whyte, Kathleen. Design in Embroidery. Newton Centre, Mass.: Branford, 1969. 240p. [C]

Intended for more advanced needleworkers, the book covers the technical aspects of embroidery, such as threads, materials, and stitches. The emphasis is on design, with discussion of shape, patterns, composition, and so on. A brief bibliography is appended for reference and further study.

456 ● Wiczyk, Arlene Zeger, ed. A Treasury of Needlepoint Projects from Godey's Lady's Book. New York: Arco, 1972. 320p. [C]

Dating from 1838 (the starting year of the magazine) until the 1890s, selected reprints from the above women's magazines, including various needlework projects, done in different techniques, are featured in this volume. The illustrations are all in black-and-white, and the text, of course, is old-fashioned. Useful for collectors or experienced needleworkers, who can utilize those patterns and apply them to modern projects.

457 ● Willcox, Donald J. New Designs in Stitchery. New
    York: Van Nostrand, 1970. 120p. [C]

An unorthodox treatment of a craft that is current-
ly enjoying a renaissance in Scandinavia. The book views
needlework as a fine art. The author explores a broad range
of stitchery thread and other materials to create unusual effects. The photographs (a few in color) are works of Scandinavian artists, with some pieces from Finnish and Swedish
museums. The various stitches are described briefly, together with other elements of design (color, material, etc.).
Not a workbook, but an informative treatment of modern
needlecraft in Scandinavia.

458 ● Williams, Elsa S. Bargello; Florentine Canvas Work.
    New York: Van Nostrand, 1967. 64p. [C]

Williams designed and adapted fifty-five new patterns, all of these are reproduced as large as possible,
some in color. A color key and suggestions for use are
provided for each. In the introductory chapter, the author
relates a short history of the bargello stitch, explaining its
origin and possible "migration" from one country to another.
Since graphs or charts are not included here, only the experienced needleworker would be able to copy the patterns
from the photographs.

459 ● Williams, Elsa S. Creative Canvas Work. New York:
    Van Nostrand, 1974. 64p. [D]

Williams treats needlework here as a means of
creative expression. For both beginners and the experienced, this book offers new possibilities. Special attention
is given to the innovative use of traditional stitches. The
detailed diagrams and many excellent illustrations, some in
color, encourage the needleworker to experiment with a variety of stitches. Additional chapters give practical advice
on blocking, enlarging, and finishing the project. Photographs show some of the uses of canvaswork in making rugs,
handbags, chair seats, and pillows.

460 ● Wilson, Erica. The Craft of Crewel Embroidery.
    Illustrated by Vladimir Kagan. New York: Scrib-
    ner, 1971. 96p. [A]

A basic book on crewel embroidery for beginners.
Forty-seven stitches are shown in easy-to-follow diagrams.
Finished projects are presented in black-and-white photographs.
The first part of the book contains the usual technical instruc-
tions--choosing fabrics, stretching and blocking, color, yarns,
needles, and so on. A good book to start crewel embroidery.

461 ● Wilson Erica.   Erica Wilson's Christmas World.
      New York: Scribner, 1980. 160p. [D]

     The well-known author of many books here pre-
sents a large variety of projects. The work is divided into
three main chapters. First, ornaments for the tree; second,
"deck the halls"; and third, miscellaneous Christmas items
suitable for gift or decoration. The techniques include crewel embroidery, needlepoint, appliqué, quilting, and making
Christmas ornaments with beads, sequins, and ribbons. All
projects are fully explained and illustrated in black-and-white
or color pictures. A rich collection of Christmas projects,
from simple to very sophisticated.

462 ● Wilson, Erica.   Fun with Crewel Embroidery.   New
      York: Scribner, 1965.   41p. [A]

     Wilson moves from simple stitches and patterns to
more complicated projects. Included is an alphabet of stitches, with photographs and drawings. Directions are given for
enlarging a design. Each project is fully illustrated with
photographs and sketches of the particular design. A good
workbook for young beginners.

463 ● Wilson, Erica.   More Needleplay. New York: Scrib-
      ner, 1979. 192p. [C]

     This book testifies the wide knowledge and versa-
tility of Erica Wilson, one of the best-known authors in the
field. This volume covers many techniques, some of them
quite unusual, such as circles (yo-yos). Each technique is
represented with a project, explained and illustrated (often
in color). Since some of the techniques are fairly difficult,
this book is not for beginners.

464 ● Wilson, Erica.   Needleplay. New York, Scribner,
      1975. 189p. [D]

The well-known designer transfers in this book twenty-six video programs into the medium of print, including over fifty stitches for crewel and needlepoint, with over thirty-five projects to work. Both beginners and needleworkers with more experience can use these instructions and patterns. Excellent graphics, photographs, and other illustrations help users to create their own designs and use their own ideas.

465 ● Wingfield, George Digby. Elizabethan Embroidery. New York: Yoseloff, 1964. 151p., 80 plates

In this historical treatment of Elizabethan embroidery the author illustrates and reviews some of the finest and best-documented pieces, using contemporary records, inventories, and portraits. The plates are photographs of the original embroidery pieces from various museums, as well as portraits of some personalities of the period. Though this is not a workbook, it will nevertheless be invaluable to students of the period.

466 ● Winter, Adalee. Needlecraft Kingdom. Birmingham, Ala.: Oxmoor, 1975. 64p. [B]

This collection of designs with very clear, easy-to-follow charts (many in color) include flowers, animals, figures, geometric patterns, and so on. Some of the finished products are shown in color. A practical, useful book for both beginners and for others with some experience.

467 ● Winter, Adalee. Needlecraft Treasury. Birmingham, Ala.: Oxmoor, 1979. 192p. [D]

Similar in format and arrangement to the author's earlier book. Winter displays many original patterns that can be used for a variety of projects, such as pillows, chair seats, game boards, rugs, and wall hangings. Alphabets and designs for special occasions are also presented. The charts are clear, in color, and easy to follow. The appendix gives technical instructions, with a dictionary of stitches. A good workbook for both beginners and the more experienced.

468 ● Winter, Adalee. Religious Designs for Needlework. Birmingham, Ala.: Oxmoor, 1977. 64p. [C]

According to the author, "There are many places in a church where needlework can be used either to enhance the beauty of the interior, or to add to the meaning of the service." She presents a large collection of religious designs, suitable for both the Christian and Judaic services. The meaning of the symbols is explained, and they are presented with charts (in color) on graph paper, making them very easy to copy. The finished products are displayed in color photographs. Technical instructions are kept to a minimum, so this is a book only for the more experienced.

469 ● Winter, Adalee. Wildflower Designs for Needlework; Charts, Histories, and Watercolors of 29 Wildflowers. Birmingham, Ala.: Oxmoor, 1979. 80p. [C]

This attractive collection of wildflowers adapted for needlepoint offers detailed charts for each flower, with color codes. Since technical instructions are kept to a minimum, only experienced needleworkers should try the fairly elaborate designs.

470 ● Witt, Susan. Classics for Needlepoint. Birmingham, Ala.: Oxmoor, 1981. 122p. [C]

The author developed a system of transferring patterns to canvas in a much simpler method than that described in any other how-to book. Different-colored pens are used to dot canvas intersections that correspond to boxes on the chart. Witt presents twenty-eight beautiful designs, mostly in Oriental style--Chinese, Indian, Turkish. Included is a list of nineteen stitches and detailed directions, color photographs, and graphs for each design. A list of suppliers and a metric chart are appended.

471 ● Woelders, Ann. Stitchery, Free Expression. Fabrics, Stitches, Designs. New York: Van Nostrand, 1973. 104p. [C]

This book demonstrates the freedom of expression possible in stitchery. The designs are all in a modernistic style, using a wide range of techniques and fabrics to create various textural effects. Technical advice is included, but the emphasis is on creativity. The illustrations are in both color and black-and-white. Not the usual workbook, but an introduction to stitchery as modern artistic expression.

472 ● Young, Eleanor R.   Crewel Embroidery (A Concise Guide). New York: Watts, 1976. 63p. [A]

After a short introductory remark about the history of embroidery, the author presents useful technical instructions concerning designs, supplies, stitches, and finishing. She also discusses ideas for original designs and the problem of enlarging patterns to the desired size. Large, easy-to-follow diagrams of the various stitches are especially helpful for beginners.

473 ● Young, Eleanor R.   Needlepoint (A Concise Guide). New York: Watts, 1976. 59p. [A]

In a book similar in format and arrangement to her other volume, Young presents basic instructions for needlepoint, including choosing the design, buying the right supplies, blocking, and finishing. The book illustrates only stitches, not finished products. However, the large diagrams of the various stitches are easy to follow and learn. A good, basic guide for beginners or young people.

474 ● Zagreb Etnografski Muzej.   Yugoslavian/Croatian Folk Embroidery; Designs and Techniques.   Foreword by Jelka Radaus Ribaric. Description of techniques by Blazenz Szenczi. Photographs by Mitja Koman. New York: Van Nostrand, 1976. 22p. [C]

A rich collection of Yugoslavian-Croatian embroidery is presented in this volume with beautiful photographs in bold colors. The text briefly discusses the history of embroidery in this part of Eastern Europe and gives a short introduction to stitches, materials, and techniques. Some 190 patterns are introduced to the experienced needleworker, giving endless possibilities for projects and applications.

475 ● Zimiles, Martha.   A Treasury of Needlework Designs. New York: Van Nostrand, 1976. 208p. [D]

This book contains 350 full-size, ready-to-copy patterns. The designs include flying, walking, and swimming figures, heraldry, sports, animals, flowers, vegetables, and so on. Since the patterns are easy to copy, detailed instructions are not included. The quality of the line drawings is not even; the animals, for example, are poorly sketched, while the flowers and leaves are excellent representations. A rich source of patterns for both beginners and experienced needleworkers.

[Numbers refer to entries.]

SUBJECT INDEX

African 436
Alphabets 57, 85, 86, 88,
118, 139, 179, 194, 344,
364, 375, 427, 438, 441,
451
American (including Colonial)
15, 29, 45, 64, 103, 127,
128, 129, 130, 193, 203,
214, 220, 239, 256, 258,
300, 335, 361, 366, 369,
420, 435, 437
American Indian 69, 90, 109,
151, 214, 259, 422
Ancient and primitive 293,
335, 361, 412
Animals 13, 56, 67, 87, 112,
150, 172 173, 184, 295,
438
Appliqué 8, 16, 19, 27, 43,
52, 59, 68, 69, 71, 75,
102, 110, 159, 164, 212,
218, 242, 268, 273, 280,
281, 291, 296, 300, 329,
342, 374, 381, 400, 405,
418, 426, 429, 461
Armed Forces 180
Art Nouveau 132

Baby's needs 268
Bargello 25, 58, 71, 82, 84,
88, 89, 91, 92, 94, 96, 97,
107, 121, 137, 145, 159,
161, 162, 179, 197, 214,
231, 234, 236, 237, 240,
241, 247, 258, 302, 312

345, 349, 362, 389, 397,
398, 401, 414, 421, 429,
458
Bible designs 238
Birds 87, 100, 173, 194, 295
Blackwork 52, 73, 141, 173,
185, 245, 247, 289, 302,
353, 379, 389, 400
Blocking see Finishing
Borders 58, 87, 150, 158,
170, 173, 194, 197, 351,
440, 443

Caucasus 243
Celebrities 190, 284, 384,
394, 395
Center designs 158
Chair covers 59, 191
Children (needlework for) 108,
149, 286, 342, 453
Chinese 63, 260, 261, 263
Christmas 126, 448, 461
Churches (needlework for) 54,
74, 134, 314, 357, 468
Clothes and linens 110, 120,
324
Crewel 7, 13, 30, 35, 45,
51, 52, 56, 59, 64, 69, 71,
73, 93, 94, 138, 159, 168,
169, 196, 212, 258, 276,
289, 300, 311, 345, 348,
353, 375, 376, 380, 381,
412, 419, 420, 426, 429,
437, 460, 461, 462, 463,
464, 472

151